Great Home Runs of the 20th Century

Great Home Runs of the 20th Century

Rich Westcott

Temple University Press

Philadelphia

To my mother, Ruth M. Westcott, who pointed me in the right direction, and who spent a lifetime helping, caring, and encouraging

Temple University Press, Philadelphia 19122

Published 2001
Printed in the United States of America

♾ The paper used in this publication meets the requirements of the American National Standard for Information Sciences—Permanence of Paper for Printed Library Materials, ANSI Z39.48-1984.

Library of Congress Cataloging-in-Publication Data

Westcott, Rich.
Great home runs of the 20th century / Rich Westcott.
p. cm.
Includes bibliographical references.
ISBN 1-56639-858-4 (cloth : alk. paper)
1. Home runs (Baseball)—United States—History. 2. Baseball players—United States. 3. Baseball—Records—United States. I. Title.
GV868.4.W48 2001
796.357'0973—dc21 00-061981

Contents

Introduction

Ask just about any baseball fan to name five major league players—past or present—and the answer is predictable. Virtually everyone answers with the names of power hitters.

No singles hitters are mentioned. No base stealers or defensive wizards make the list. Seldom, in fact, does anyone name a famous pitcher. Despite their obvious abilities, these kinds of players simply don't rate on the same level as the big sluggers who hit the ball out of the park.

Home run hitters. They are the players who rank foremost in the minds of most people who follow baseball. They are the ones who provide the excitement, the ones people talk about.

People respond the way they do, of course, with good reason. The home run offers the single most exciting moment in baseball. No other incident that occurs on a regular basis provides even close to the same kind of thrill or admiration as the home run.

It takes no more than a look back to the 1998 and 1999 seasons to confirm that point. Particularly in 1998, while Mark McGwire and Sammy Sosa chased the most hallowed record in baseball, a whole world watched, a whole world quivered with excitement, and baseball once again became the most popular game on the planet after a strike had soured the public on it for several years.

It was all because of the home run. All because of those majestic drives, coming as they do in various forms, that with one swing of the bat can change the whole complexion of a game or even a season.

There is nothing more symbolic of the popularity of the home run than the realization that most people would rather see a 10–8 game filled with homers than a 2–1 pitchers' duel. The chance of seeing a home run is what brings many people these days to the ball park, and it is what gets them jumping out of their seats and cheering.

In cities throughout the National League, ballpark attendance figures swelled dramatically when either McGwire or Sosa came to town in '98 and

'99. An excellent example of this phenomenon was seen in Philadelphia in August 1999. Nearly 50,000 fans—more than double the number the Phillies had been drawing—flocked to Veterans Stadium when McGwire and the St. Louis Cardinals visited for a meaningless series. Much of the crowd arrived early just to watch McGwire take batting practice.

On a historic level, many of the most memorable events in baseball have involved home runs. Naturally, there are some no-hitters, some unassisted triple plays, some great catches, and other spectacular feats that rank among the sport's finest moments. But dramatic home runs dominate the list. In fact, in a survey by *Baseball America,* readers chose home runs as four of the five most memorable moments in baseball history.

How can any compilation of baseball's most memorable occasions not include Bobby Thomson's legendary "Shot Heard 'Round the World"? Or Bill Mazeroski's famous World Series clincher? Or McGwire's 70th homer, Hank Aaron's 715th, or scores of other incomparable four-baggers?

It is not possible to rate these feats in any place except at the top of baseball's most glorious single accomplishments. Without question, nothing else poses a threat.

In recognition of these heroic feats, I have written *Great Home Runs of the 20th Century* to chronicle the 30 most dramatic homers in the last 100 years. I have also cited the top 10 All-Star Game home runs as well as 60 other noteworthy homers, bringing the total to the top 100 homers in baseball history.

The 30 most memorable homers, many hit by Hall of Famers and most by highly prominent players, were selected not only because of their dramatic flavor, but also because they all had a significant impact on the situations in which they were hit and in most cases on the sport of baseball as a whole.

The contents of the book, therefore, do not just include a collection of great home runs. These 30 homers are the biggest ones ever hit.

And each one is unique. There have been no others like them. Each has its own special characteristics and in its own way is vastly different from all the rest.

For that reason, most home run feats that were matched by others are not included in the book.

Not mentioned either are memorable minor league home runs, not the least of which was one that some call the shortest homer in professional baseball history. Although there is disagreement over whether or not the event ever happened, the homer was a smash that according to some accounts was said to have traveled all of two feet off the bat of Andy Oyler of the Minneapolis Millers during a game in 1900 that was being played in a driving rainstorm. The ball landed in a huge mud puddle in front of the plate, and while opposing players vainly searched for the horsehide, Oyler circled the bases. If the claim is true, it was certainly one of the most unusual homers ever hit.

But that's a story for another time. For now, we're going to travel through baseball history to look at the greatest major league home runs of all time and the men who hit them. Each was a truly remarkable feat.

Frank Baker

The Home Run Achieves New Status

October 16, 1911 Shibe Park

The first time a home run attracted substantial attention in baseball it was such a captivating event that the hitter was given a special nickname. From that moment on, he became known as "Home Run."

Frank (Home Run) Baker was the only big league player ever to carry that sobriquet. It was a label that was well deserved.

Baker was not only one of the first home run hitters of note. When he hit home runs on successive days against two future Hall of Fame pitchers in the 1911 World Series, he pioneered a major change in the way baseball people viewed the home run. Thereafter, the home run began to gain wider recognition as a major offensive weapon in a game that had previously focused on moving runners along one base at a time.

Before Baker, there had, of course, been plenty of home runs. But in the dead-ball era, the home run still occurred infrequently, and when it did, it was not considered a major part of a team's arsenal.

Runs were scored by a technique then called the "inside game." Today, it is called "the little man's game." Runs were scratched out one at a time using well-placed singles or doubles, stolen bases, bunts, and whatever else could be employed to move the runner along.

Although it eventually took the prodigious clouting of Babe Ruth to fully change that approach and to end the dead-ball era, Baker's home runs began to push baseball in that direction. No one before the slugging third baseman of the Philadelphia Athletics had done such a thing, even though there were a number of redoubtable sluggers.

One of the main reasons the credit goes to Baker is that his hitting occurred in the spotlight of a World Series. The future Hall of Famer was not the first batter to hit more than one homer in the Series, but the circumstances made his efforts more noticeable.

Baker was already a prominent slugger. After joining the Athletics late in the 1908 season, he had begun his rookie campaign with a grand slam in his first at-bat in the first inning of the opening game in 1909. That not only gave the A's a 4–1 victory over Boston, but it was the only grand slam of Baker's career.

As the new hot corner custodian, Baker, an excellent fielder, joined an infield that also included Stuffy McInnis at first, Eddie Collins at second, and Jack Barry at shortstop. The group became known as the "$100,000 infield," a tag that would be spoken in awe over the ensuing years.

In 1910, Baker's .409 batting average led the Athletics to their first World Series victory as they stunned the Chicago Cubs in five games. The following year, Philadelphia was back in the Series for the third time since the American League began in 1901. (There was no World Series when the Athletics won their first pennant in 1902.)

Baker had a banner year in 1911. He hit .334 and drove in 115 runs. He also clubbed 11 homers to win what would be his first of four consecutive home run crowns and the seventh four-bagger title for an A's hitter in 11 years. (Harry Davis had won four, preceded by Nap Lajoie and Socks Seybold, each with one.)

Connie Mack's A's had stormed to the American League pennant with 101 wins, good for a 13 ½-game lead over the hated Detroit Tigers. Baker, who after being spiked by Ty Cobb the previous year and attacked the Tigers' star, causing a near riot, was not the A's only big hitter. Collins, McInnis, Danny Murphy, and Bris Lord all hit over .300. On the mound, Jack Coombs won 29 games, Eddie Plank 22, and Chief Bender 17.

As formidable as they were, the A's, who tied for the league lead in home runs with 35, had all they could handle as they faced the National

Frank Baker gave the home run new status with his pair of Series swats.

League winner, the New York Giants. John McGraw's club, led by 26-game winner Christy Mathewson and 24-game winner Rube Marquard, had won 99 games, finishing 7 ½ games ahead of the second-place Cubs. The Giants led the National League in hitting with a .279 average, but of greater significance, had set a major league record (which still stands) for stolen bases with 347. New York outfielders Fred Snodgrass, Josh Devore, and Red Murray had combined for 160 of those steals.

McGraw outfitted his team in black uniforms for the Series. In the first game, Mathewson outdueled Bender, winning 2–1, at New York's Polo Grounds. Baker had two singles and scored the Athletics' only run.

The Series switched to Philadelphia's Shibe Park for the second game two days later. A crowd of 26,286 overflowed the park to watch Marquard toe the rubber against Plank in the second straight battle of future Hall of Fame pitchers.

Another brilliant duel ensued. The A's got one run in the first inning on a single by Lord, an error, a sacrifice, and a wild pitch. But the Giants tied the count in the second when A's outfielder Rube Oldring misjudged a drive by Buck Herzog that fell for a double. Herzog then scored on a single by Chief Meyers.

The 1–1 deadlock stood until the sixth inning. With two outs, Collins doubled. Baker was next, and with his huge 52-ounce bat, he drilled a Marquard fastball over the 12-foot-high right-field wall for a two-run homer. The blast held up, and the A's walked off with a 3–1 win to even the Series. But the sparks were just beginning to fly.

A relatively new feature had been applied to the 1911 Series. A number of players on both sides, as well as Mack and McGraw, were having their opinions recorded by ghostwriters in columns in various New York and Philadelphia newspapers.

After Baker's home run, a column bearing Mathewson's byline appeared in a New York newspaper. The Giants star berated Marquard for pitching carelessly to the A's third sacker and for disregarding McGraw's pregame clubhouse instructions not to throw a fastball to Baker.

Having said that, Mathewson then went out the next day to face the A's and Coombs back at the Polo Grounds. The Giants took an early 1–0 lead with an unearned run in the third. The margin stood until Baker came to bat with one out in the top of the ninth.

Just two outs away from victory, Mathewson, who had allowed only one run in 44 ⅓ previous World Series innings, got ahead in the count 0–2. On the next pitch, Baker crushed Mathewson's delivery into the lower right-field stands. Stunned Giants fans watched in silence as Frank circled the bases.

Two innings later, with one out, Collins singled and Baker beat out an infield hit. Both moved up a base on Herzog's wild throw. An error by Art Fletcher and a single by Davis gave the A's two runs, which more than offset an unearned run by the Giants in the bottom of the 11th.

The A's had a 4–2 victory. Now it was time for Marquard's ghostwriter to go to bat. "Will the great Mathewson tell us exactly what pitch he made to Baker?" the column blared. "I seem to remember that he was present at the same clubhouse meeting at which Mr. McGraw discussed Baker's weakness. Could it be that Matty, too, let go a careless pitch when it meant the ballgame for our side? Or maybe Baker just doesn't have a weakness."

At least McGraw was starting to feel that way. "I don't know what to do about him," the Giants manager said. "We just can't seem to get him out when we have to."

Baker's two home runs made him the toast of the baseball world. He was a national celebrity. Suddenly, he was no longer Frank. He was given a new name of "Home Run." It would stay with him the rest of his life.

The Athletics cleanup hitter belted no more home runs in the Series. But his bat stayed alive. The Series was delayed for six straight days because of rain, and when it resumed the A's won two out of the next three, including a 13–2 rout in the deciding sixth game, to capture the Series. Baker had two hits each in two of the final three games, and finished the Series with a glittering .375 average.

Baker's hitting heroics continued the next year when after getting a raise to $8,500, he blistered American League pitching with a .347 average. He drove in 133, scored 116, and among his 200 hits were 40 doubles, 21 triples, and a league-leading 10 home runs.

In what was surely the A's greatest era—they won four pennants in five years between 1910 and 1914 and six flags overall since 1901—Baker continued his lusty hitting. He homered off Marquard to help the A's to a 6–4 win in the first game of the 1913 World Series while hitting .450 in the five-game set, again won by the A's.

Baker, who sat out both the 1915 and 1920 seasons because of contract disputes, finished his 13-year big league career, which ended in 1921 with the New York Yankees, with a .307 average, 96 home runs, and 1,013 RBI. After his playing days, he became a manager at Easton, Maryland, in the Eastern Shore League. There he discovered a 17-year-old slugger named Jimmie Foxx and convinced Mack that he should be signed by the A's.

Mack knew what he had in Foxx, and he knew what he had in Baker. "If he had played with the livelier ball, he would have rivaled Ruth," Mack said about Frank many years later. "He hit the fence dozens of times, and those shots would have carried over the wall today."

Baker was said to have hit the fence 38 times in 1912 alone. His best shots, though, were the two that carried over the fence in the 1911 World Series, and gave him the name of Home Run Baker.

New York	**AB**	**R**	**H**	**RBI**	**Philadelphia**	**AB**	**R**	**H**	**RBI**
Devore, lf	4	0	0	0	Lord, lf	4	1	1	0
Doyle, 2b	4	0	0	0	Oldring, cf	3	0	0	0
Snodgrass, cf	3	0	2	0	Collins, 2b	3	1	2	0
Murray, rf	4	0	0	0	Baker, 3b	3	1	1	2
Merckle, 1b	3	0	1	0	Murphy, rf	3	0	0	0
Herzog, 3b	3	1	1	0	Davis, 1b	3	0	0	0
Fletcher, ss	3	0	0	0	Barry, ss	3	0	0	0
Meyers, c	3	0	1	1	Thomas, c	3	0	0	0
Marquard, p	2	0	0	0	Plank, p	3	0	0	0
Crandall, p	1	0	0	0					
Totals	30	1	5	1		28	3	4	2

New York	0	1	0	0	0	0	0	0	0	**1**
Philadelphia	1	0	0	0	0	2	0	0	x	**3**

New York	**IP**	**H**	**R**	**ER**	**BB**	**SO**
Marquard (L)	7	4	3	2	0	4
Crandall	1	0	0	0	0	2
Philadelphia	**IP**	**H**	**R**	**ER**	**BB**	**SO**
Plank (W)	9	5	1	1	0	8

E–Devore, Murray, Merkle. LOB–New York 3, Philadelphia 2. 2B–Herzog, Collins. HR–Baker. SH–Oldring. HBP–By Plank (Snodgrass). WP–Marquard. U–Connolly, Brennan, Klem, Dinneen. T–1:52. A–26,286.

Babe Ruth

A Record That Stands the Test of Time

September 30, 1927 Yankee Stadium

The great home runs of baseball have had varying impacts on the game. Some have been more pronounced than others. A few have had an extremely high level of significance.

Then there was the home run hit by Babe Ruth on the next-to-last day of the 1927 season at Yankee Stadium. It stands alone as the most influential home run in baseball history.

The home run was Ruth's 60th circuit clout of the season, and it set a standard for home run hitting that every future power hitter was measured against and a level at which every power hitter thereafter aimed. And it established a home run record that stood for the next 34 years.

Ruth revolutionized the offensive part of baseball by changing the game from one that emphasized the plodding process of scoring by wit, guile, and the act of moving along one base at a time to a game that focused on the home run. Before Ruth came along to win 12 home run crowns and hit 714 four-baggers during his career, the home run had been merely an incidental part of a team's offense. After his conversion from a pitcher to a full-time position player, the home run became the major offensive weapon in baseball.

With his 60th homer, **Babe Ruth** reached a level never before attained.

The big lefthander had brought baseball to this point in stages. He had set new home run records with 29 in 1919, with 54 in 1920, and with 59 in 1921. By that time, he was no longer a star pitcher and part-time outfielder with the Boston Red Sox. He was an everyday right fielder with the New York Yankees.

He was also well on his way to becoming the biggest single name in baseball history, a man who not only popularized the home run on the field, but one who was watched and idolized by legions of fans off the field. They joyously called him The Bambino and The Sultan of Swat, and when Yankee Stadium opened in 1923, it quickly was crowned The House That Ruth Built.

Although his celebrity status and his endless encounters with the good life took a heavy toll on his body, Ruth remained an awesome hitter through the mid-1920s, hitting .393 in 1923, .378 in 1924, and .372 in 1926. But his home run totals sloughed off to mere mortal levels. In 1926, his 47 homers were his highest total since 1921.

The Babe was primed for a banner season in 1927. He had put in a busy winter, spending 22 weeks on a vaudeville tour that took him from Minnesota to Southern California, and another 22 days making a movie in Hollywood. He watched his diet, got lots of rest, and ran five miles each day. When he reported to spring training, having just signed a three-year contract calling for an annual salary of $70,000, he was in his best shape in years.

The team that surrounded Ruth in 1927 was arguably the best ever to set foot on a baseball diamond. Although they had lost the 1926 World Series to the St. Louis Cardinals in seven games, the Yanks had won three American League pennants and one World Series earlier in the decade.

The '27 club was the best of the group. With an offense dubbed Murderers' Row, which included such heavy hitters as Ruth, Lou Gehrig, Bob Meusel, Tony Lazzeri, and Earle Combs, the Yanks were simply unstoppable as they roared to the American League pennant with 110 victories and a massive 19-game lead over the Philadelphia Athletics. As one writer put it, "This isn't a race, it's a landslide." The might of the Yanks was demonstrated further when they erased the National League champion Pittsburgh Pirates in four games in the World Series.

The focal point of the season, though, was Ruth. Spurred by Gehrig batting in the cleanup spot in the Yankees batting order, the Babe enjoyed a season of long-distance clouting that would not be matched until Roger Maris came along to hit 61 homers in 1961.

Ruth had started the season slowly. He didn't get his first home run until the fourth game of the season when he mashed a pitch by the Athletics' Howard Ehmke into the stands. By the end of April, Babe had just four home runs.

He hit 12 in May. Then he added nine in June. But Gehrig was the league's home run leader, and Ruth was just the trailer.

Ruth added nine more homers in July and nine in August. He had 43 four-baggers as he entered the final month of September. Gehrig, in his third full season, still held the lead with 44.

Babe began September with the 400th home run of his career, a shot off the Athletics' Rube Walberg. It was the fourth time in 1927 that Walberg had surrended a homer to the Yankees slugger, and it pulled Ruth even with Gehrig.

On September 6, Ruth exploded with three home runs against Boston to take the lead from Gehrig for the first time all season. It was the Babe's only three-homer day of the campaign.

The next day, he added two more homers against Red Sox pitching to bring his total for the year to 49. Four days went by before Ruth reached 50. Then he continued to add to his total, and on September 27 he blasted a grand slam—his only one of the season—off Philadelphia's Lefty Grove. That gave Ruth 57 home runs with three games left in the season.

Ruth tied his own record in the 153rd game when he homered twice for the eighth time during the season in a game with the Washington Senators. He touched Hod Lisenbee for the first clout and Paul Hopkins for the second one as the Yanks romped to an easy 15–4 victory before a scant Yankee Stadium crowd of 5,000.

Baseball fans throughout the country were closely following Ruth's exploits as the Yankees' season came down to its last two games (the club played 155 games in 1927 with one being a tie). The Babe needed just one homer to reach the magic and theretofore considered unreachable total of 60.

Lefthander Tom Zachary was on the mound for the Senators, facing the Yankees George Pipgras. Zachary, who had a 4–6 record for the third-place Nats, had earlier in the season served up home runs number 22 and 36 to Ruth, the former coming while the hurler was still a member of the Browns.

Zachary walked Ruth in their first encounter in the first inning. The next two times to the plate, Ruth lashed singles.

Washington took a 2–0 lead in the fourth inning when Muddy Ruel and Ossie Bluege each singled in runs. In the bottom of the fourth, Ruth singled, went to third on a single by Gehrig and scored on a fly to left by Meusel. Ruth scored again in the sixth after lacing a two-out single and coming around on hits by Gehrig and Meusel.

The score was still tied at 2–2 as the game moved into the bottom of the eighth. Still pitching, Zachary retired Combs, but then surrendered a triple to left by Mark Koenig. Ruth was the next batter.

In what turned out to be his final at-bat of the game, Ruth took a called strike on the first pitch, then a ball high and away. On the third offering, Zachary tried to sneak a low curve past the mighty slugger.

Ruth turned on it and sent a high, towering fly to deep right. The ball was curving toward the foul line, but stayed fair long enough to go into the stands in fair territory for home run number 60 and a 4–2 Yankees lead. Zachary screamed, "Foul ball, foul ball," but to no avail.

"I don't say it was the best curve anybody ever threw, but it was as good as any I ever threw," said Zachary, who had argued with the umpire, then angrily fired his glove in the air after the hit.

Ruth stood briefly at the plate and watched the flight of the ball. Then, as the 10,000 spectators flung their hats in the air and roared their approval, he chugged merrily around the bases. As he did, Yankees players pounded their bats on the wooden floor of the dugout.

Ruth was greeted at home, first by Gehrig and then by the rest of the Yankee team. When the Babe went to right field at the top of the ninth inning, he was met by a deafening cheer from the crowd. Ruth responded by doing a brisk military march to his position. It was the climax of one of the greatest days the game of baseball had ever seen.

In the Yankees clubhouse after the game, Ruth chanted, "Sixty, count 'em, sixty. Let's see some other SOB match that." Babe and his teammates celebrated his feat far into the night. Ruth went 0-for-3 in the season's final game.

Later, Ruth would pay tribute to Gehrig, the man who hit behind him in the lineup. "I don't think I ever would have established my home run record if it hadn't been for Lou," he said. "He was really getting his beef behind the ball that season. Pitchers began pitching to me because if they passed me, they still had Lou to contend with."

Although Ruth had many other noteworthy achievements, he reached the high point of his career on that late September afternoon when he hit what was then the unfathomable total of 60 home runs in a single season. At the time, it would have been hard to find anyone willing to suggest that that total would ever be reached again.

Washington	**AB**	**R**	**H**	**RBI**	**New York**	**AB**	**R**	**H**	**RBI**
Rice, rf	3	0	1	0	Combs, cf	4	0	0	0
Harris, 2b	3	0	0	0	Koenig, ss	4	1	1	0
Ganzel, cf	4	0	1	0	Ruth, rf	3	3	3	2
Goslin, lf	4	1	1	0	Gehrig, 1b	4	0	2	0
Judge, 1b	4	0	0	0	Meusel, lf	3	0	1	2
Ruel, c	2	1	1	1	Lazzeri, 2b	3	0	0	0
Bluege, 3b	3	0	1	1	Dugan, 3b	3	0	1	0
Gillis, ss	4	0	0	0	Bengough, c	3	0	1	0
Zachary, p	2	0	0	0	Pipgras, p	2	0	0	0
Johnson, ph	1	0	0	0	Pennock, p	1	0	0	0
Totals	30	2	5	2		30	4	9	4

Washington	0	0	0	2	0	0	0	0	0	**2**
New York	0	0	0	1	0	1	0	2	x	**4**

Washington	**IP**	**H**	**R**	**ER**	**BB**	**SO**
Zachary (L)	8	9	4	4	1	1
New York	**IP**	**H**	**R**	**ER**	**BB**	**SO**
Pipgras	6	4	2	2	5	0
Pennock (W)	3	1	0	0	1	0

E–Gehrig. DP–Washington 2. LOB–Washington 7, New York 4. 2B–Rice. 3B–Koenig. HR–Ruth. SB–Ruel, Bluege, Rice. SH–Muesel. HBP–By Pipgras (Rice). T–1:38. A–10,000.

Babe Ruth

Did He Really Call the Shot?

October 1, 1932 Wrigley Field

Of all the home runs hit over the course of major league baseball's long history, none was—and remains to this day—more controversial than Babe Ruth's legendary "Called Shot" of 1932.

Did he or didn't he call the home run he hit at Wrigley Field in the third game of the World Series between the New York Yankees and Chicago Cubs? That is a question that has never been precisely answered but has led to countless hours of lively debate since that October 1, 1932, afternoon.

Ruth was then on the back side of what was a glorious 22-year career. The man they called The Bambino had hit .341 during the '32 season while clubbing 41 home runs, driving in 137, and scoring 120.

For most people, that kind of season would have sent them into fits of ecstacy. For the Babe, though, it was just another year in a long line of great years. Despite such glittering figures, he failed to lead the American League in any of the major offensive categories, and his streak of six straight home run crowns came to an end in 1932.

Still, with Ruth teaming with future Hall of Famers Lou Gehrig, Bill Dickey, Tony Lazzeri, and Earle Combs—each of whom hit .300 or higher—the '32 Yankees represented one of the great clubs ever to step onto the diamond. With three pitchers (Red Ruffing, Lefty Gomez, and Herb Pennock) also destined for the Hall of Fame, the Yanks had cruised to the American League pennant, winning 107 games (while losing just 47) and ending the three-year reign of the Philadelphia Athletics, who finished a distant second, 13 games back.

For Ruth, it would be his last World Series. But for the Yankees, it would be their first of five trips to the autumn spectacular during the 1930s. All would end in Yankees victories.

The opposing Cubs were no strangers to the Series, either. They had last appeared in it in a losing venture with the Athletics in 1929, and would show up again in 1935 and 1938, losing each time.

The '32 Bruins were possibly the weakest of that group of Chicago pennant winners. Posting a modest 90–64 record, the Cubs had one of the lowest percentages (.584) a team ever took to the Series. It paled by comparison to the Yanks' gaudy .695 mark.

Chicago had stumbled along much of the season in second place under unpopular manager Rogers Hornsby. But after Cubs president William Veeck jetisoned Hornsby on August 2 and replaced him with jocular first baseman Charlie Grimm, the club caught fire. Following a streak of 20 wins in 21 games, the Cubs finished in first place, four games ahead of the Pittsburgh Pirates.

Still, the Cubs were no match for the Yankee juggernaut. With Gehrig slamming a two-run homer in the first game and adding three hits in the second, the Yanks beat them 12–6 and 5–2 in the first two games of the Series at Yankee Stadium.

The teams harbored a healthy dislike for each other, and as soon as the Series began, so did the razzing. Contributing to the bad blood was the fact that Yankees manager Joe McCarthy had been dumped unceremoniously by the Cubs during the 1930 season and made no secret that he wanted revenge.

More significantly, New York players were especially incensed that the Cubs had voted former Yankee shortstop, Mark Koenig—who had come to Chicago late in the season and played exceptionally well, hitting .353 down the stretch—only a one-half share of the Series money. The Yanks rode the Cubs unmercifully, accusing the Chicago players of being stingy and cheapskates. Ruth was particularly boisterous, maligning the Cubs every chance he got.

The Cubs, of course, retaliated in kind. They made Ruth their particular target, taunting him with unfriendly barbs about his oversized stomach, his heritage, and virtually every other unflattering remark they could come up with. When the teams relocated to Chicago, Cubs fans got into the act, spitting at Ruth and his wife Claire as they entered their hotel, then pelting the Babe with lemons as he stood in the outfield during batting practice before the third game.

Ruth, who was making his first visit to Wrigley Field, answered by hitting nine home runs in batting practice. "I'd play for half my salary if I could hit in this dump all the time," he bellowed to the Cubs.

As the war of words escalated into a series of ugly exchanges and actions, the setting for the third game was anything but congenial. And with a crowd of 49,986 in attendance, the venom became even thicker after Ruth smacked a titanic three-run homer in the first inning off the Cubs' Charlie Root.

Chicago, however, fought back and after four innings had pulled to a 4–4 tie. The stage was thus set for Ruth's controversial home run.

As he crouched in the on-deck circle in the top of the fifth inning, Ruth was showered with boos and jeers from the stands. Some lemons and other garbage were hurled in his direction. Then, amid a chorus of insults led by pitchers Guy Bush, Burleigh Grimes, and Pat Malone from the Cubs bench, the Babe came to bat with one out.

As he stalked to the plate, Ruth gave the choke sign to the Chicago dugout, then said to catcher Gabby Hartnett, "If that bum throws one in here, I'll hit it over the fence again."

Root's first pitch was a called strike. As the jeering intensified, Ruth looked over at the Cubs bench, raised one finger, and according to his own account years later, yelled, "Strike one."

The Cubs pitcher then threw two balls, followed by a second called strike that sent the Cubs bench into a frenzy. Bush jumped out of the dugout onto the grass and yelled at Ruth. Grimes and the others were also screaming from the top of the dugout steps. Ruth waved them back, held up two fingers, and hollered, "It only takes one to hit it out."

According to Gehrig, kneeling in the on-deck circle, Ruth and Root began yelling back and forth with the Babe finally roaring, "I'm going to knock the next pitch down your goddamn throat." Then, as legend has it, Ruth pointed to the center-field bleachers.

Root threw Ruth a change-up, and Babe lined it into the stands in right-center. Moments after Ruth had rounded the bases, laughing uproariously as he ran, Gehrig hit his second homer of the game, and the Yankees went on to a 7–5 victory with George Pipgras getting the decision. The following day, they wrapped up the Series with a 13–6 win.

Did Ruth really call the shot? Some say he did, some say he didn't.

Cubs center fielder Johnny Moore, over whose outstretched glove the homer flew, said many years later that he wasn't sure. "He really hit it, I know that," Moore recalled. "I ran as far as I could to the fence, and it was well over my head. But I can't say whether Ruth pointed or not. Both teams were really razzing each other. Our bench was riding Ruth, and he was answering them right back."

Root, who years later was still so miffed that he refused to play himself in the movie *The Babe Ruth Story,* claimed Ruth didn't call the shot. He admitted that Ruth raised his arm, but was pointing it in the pitcher's direction. "If Ruth had pointed to the center-field stands, I'd have knocked him on his fanny with the next pitch, believe me," he said.

Most of the other Cubs—one exception being reserve catcher Zack Taylor, who said, "I saw it happen. He pointed to direct center field"—denied that the gesture had actually happened. But many Yankees claimed it did.

Among them was Gehrig. "What do you think of that big monkey calling his shot, and then taking two strikes and then hitting the ball exactly where he had pointed?" he said at dinner that night with sportswriter Fred Lieb.

Ruffing also voted for Ruth. "There was no doubt," he said. "He was pointing to center field as if to say he was going to hit one there."

Writers who covered the game were conspicuously vague in their reporting of the called shot. While they mentioned it in guarded terms, only Joe Williams of the *New York World–Telegram* asserted for sure that the Babe called the shot.

As for Ruth himself, he often altered his story when asked about the shot in the years after it happened. Sometimes he acknowledged it; sometimes he denied it. Near his death in 1948, he said, "Nobody but a fool would have done what I did that day." Another time, he said, "After I hit it, I was just laughing to myself and thinking what a lucky bum I was. I called a home run and got away with it." And still one other time, he said, "I know I didn't [do it], but it made a helluva story, didn't it?"

That it did. One of the best home run stories ever told.

Babe Ruth may or may not have called the shot in the 1932 World Series.

New York	**AB**	**R**	**H**	**RBI**	**Chicago**	**AB**	**R**	**H**	**RBI**
Combs, cf	5	1	0	0	Herman, 2b	4	1	0	0
Sewell, 3b	2	1	0	0	English, 3b	4	0	0	0
Ruth, lf	4	2	2	4	Cuyler, rf	4	1	3	2
Gehrig, 1b	5	2	2	2	Stephenson, lf	4	0	1	0
Lazzeri, 2b	4	1	0	0	Moore, cf	3	1	0	0
Dickey, c	4	0	1	0	Grimm, 1b	4	0	1	1
Chapman, rf	4	0	2	1	Hartnett, c	4	1	1	1
Crosetti, ss	4	0	1	0	Jurges, ss	4	1	3	0
Pipgras, p	5	0	0	0	Root, p	2	0	0	0
Pennock, p	0	0	0	0	Malone, p	0	0	0	0
					Gudat, ph	1	0	0	0
					May, p	0	0	0	0
					Tinning, p	0	0	0	0
					Koenig, ph	0	0	0	0
					Hemsley, ph	1	0	0	0
Totals	37	7	8	7		35	5	9	4

New York 3 0 1 0 2 0 0 0 1 **7**
Chicago 1 0 2 1 0 0 0 0 1 **5**

New York	**IP**	**H**	**R**	**ER**	**BB**	**SO**
Pipgras* (W)	8	9	5	4	3	1
Pennock	1	0	0	0	0	1

Chicago	**IP**	**H**	**R**	**ER**	**BB**	**SO**
Root (L)	4⅓	6	6	5	3	4
Malone	2⅔	1	0	0	1	4
May	1⅓	1	1	0	0	1
Tinning	⅔	0	0	0	0	1

*Pitched to two batters in ninth.

E–Lazzeri, Herman, Hartnett, Jurges. DP–New York 1, Chicago 1. LOB–New York 11, Chicago 6. 2B–Chapman, Cuyler, Jurges, Grimm. HR–Ruth 2, Gehrig 2, Cuyler, Hartnett. SB–Jurges. HBP–By May (Sewell). T–2:11. A–49,986

Mel Ott

Extra-Inning Blast Wins Series

October 7, 1933 Griffith Stadium

It would take some stretch of the imagination to picture one of baseball's most memorable home runs as being hit by a little guy with an unorthodox swing who didn't have a mean bone in his body and who never played a day in the minors. That's an unlikely description, quite the opposite of the usual image of the big, strong, muscular power hitter.

If the description was used to paint a picture of Mel Ott, though, it would be right on the money. The New York Giants' stellar right fielder was all of those things and more.

Ott was one of the premier power hitters of his or any other day. And when he hit a home run in the 10th inning of the fifth game to give the Giants the clinching victory over the Washington Senators in the 1933 World Series, his name joined the list of the game's most memorable home run hitters.

On that October 7 afternoon at Washington's Griffith Stadium, Ott was just 24 years old, a mere babe by memorable home run standards. Yet, he was already a veteran of eight big league seasons and was well on his way to becoming the first National League player to hit more than 500 homers in a career.

By power-hitter standards, Ott was a shrimp. He stood just 5–9 and weighed only 170 pounds. A lefthanded batter, he lifted his right leg well off the ground when he was preparing to swing, holding it in the air for a brief moment before returning it to the ground as he launched into his beautifully fluid stroke.

So unusual was the swing but so formidable was Ott in using it that grizzled Giants manager John McGraw refused to send the plucky kid to the minors after he was signed as a 16-year-old in 1925. "No minor league manager is going to ruin him by changing his style," McGraw insisted. "He's staying with me. He's got the best natural swing I've ever seen."

So Ott never spent a day in the minors, getting to play in 35 games and hitting .383 as a teenage rookie in his first season in 1926. He would go on to spend 22 seasons in the major leagues—all with one team—hitting 511 home runs and tallying a .304 lifetime batting average during a storied career that in 1951 put him in the Hall of Fame.

Ott, who was originally a catcher before McGraw converted him to an outfielder to save his legs, was a six-time National League home run champion. While aided by the short 257-foot distance down the right-field line at New York's Polo Grounds, Ott, a dead pull-hitter who poked 323 of his four-baggers there, hit 30 or more home runs eight times, getting as high as 42 in 1929. That total tied Rogers Hornsby for the highest number of home runs ever hit in the National League.

Unlike some power hitters smitten with the killer instinct, Mel was a quietly charming fellow with an extremely mild-mannered temperament. Ott, in fact, provided the inspiration for Brooklyn Dodgers manager Leo Durocher's famous comment "Nice guys finish last."

There was no finishing last in 1933 for Ott or his Giants. Although Mel, a fine defensive player with an excellent arm who seldom sat out a game, slumped to a .283 average with 23 home runs and 103 RBI, New York, playing for the first full year under manager Bill Terry (who had succeeded the ailing McGraw), swept into first place on June 10 and held the lead the rest of the way, finishing five games ahead of the Pittsburgh Pirates.

During the season, Giants lefthander Carl Hubbell hurled 10 shutouts, including a 1–0 win over the St. Louis Cardinals in 18 innings. Hubbell, a 23-game winner and owner of a 1.66 ERA that year, also tossed a record 45⅓ consecutive scoreless innings.

The 1933 season had numerous other noteworthy events, making it one of baseball's most glorious campaigns. For the only time in baseball

An unorthodox swing couldn't keep **Mel Ott** from hitting a Series-winning blast.

history, both the American and National Leagues had Triple Crown winners in the same city in Jimmie Foxx and Chuck Klein, respectively. The first All-Star Game was played that year. Lou Gehrig broke Everett Scott's endurance record of having played in 1,308 straight games. And, in deference to the Depression, Commissioner Kenesaw Mountain Landis attempted to set an example for others by taking a 40 percent pay cut.

In the American League, Washington had followed the lead of 26-year-old rookie playing-manager Joe Cronin, who hit .309 and drove in 118 runs, to romp to the pennant. With a team that featured such standouts as Goose Goslin, Heinie Manush, Joe Kuhel, and Buddy Myer, plus 24-game winner Alvin Crowder and 22-game winner Earl Whitehill, the Senators won 99 games and finished seven games ahead of a New York Yankees team which in that period was regarded as one of the strongest clubs ever to take the field.

The Giants couldn't match the Senators in offense, but were nonetheless a formidable foe because of a glittering pitching staff that in addition to Hubbell included 19-game winner Hal Schumacher, Roy Parmelee, Freddie Fitzsimmons, and 43-year-old reliever Dolf Luque.

The Senators and Giants had met once before, in the 1924 World Series. For Washington, the '33 flag would represent the last the team ever captured, while for New York, the pennant that year would be the first of three won during the 1930s.

The experts predicted that good pitching would beat good hitting. And they were right, as the Giants quickly jumped out to a two-game lead. Hubbell fired a five-hitter to give his club a 4–2 win in the opener. Ott slammed four hits in four trips to the plate, driving in three runs with a two-run homer and an RBI single.

Schumacher fashioned another five-hitter in Game 2 as the Giants captured a 6–1 decision. Then a third straight five-hitter was delivered in Game 3, this time with Whitehill doing the honors in a 4–0 Senators triumph. Outstanding pitching was again featured in the fourth game with Hubbell going 11 innings to gain a 2–1 decision on Blondy Ryan's game-winning single.

Now one win away from their first World Series victory since 1922, the Giants sent Schumacher to the mound to tie down the big prize. A crowd of 28,454 herded into Griffith Stadium to see if Crowder could stem the tide for the Senators.

That outcome didn't seem likely as the Giants jumped out to a 3–0 lead with the help of Schumacher's two-run single in the second inning and Gus Mancuso's run-scoring double in the sixth.

Schumacher retired the first two batters in the bottom of the sixth, but then was touched for singles by Manush and Cronin. Then Fred Schulte came to the plate. Schulte, obtained during the off-season from the St. Louis Browns, brought the fans to their feet with a three-run homer to left to tie the score.

Before the sixth inning was over, not only Crowder but also Schumacher had departed. The game was left in the hands of relievers Luque for the Giants and Jack Russell for the Senators. Neither reliever budged for the next three innings. With the score still tied at 3–3, extra innings beckoned.

Russell was a career reliever who pitched for six big league teams. Later, he became a businessman and civic leader in Clearwater, Florida, where the spring training park of the Philadelphia Phillies would be named after him. Jack quickly got the first two Giants, Hughie Critz and Terry, out in the top of the 10th inning.

Then the job fell to Ott. Russell got ahead in the count, 0–2, before trying to sneak one more pitch by him. But Mel, with that familiar, high-stepping stroke, pounced on the delivery and laced it into the center-field bleachers. The blast gave the Giants a 4–3 lead.

But the game wasn't over yet. Luque had to get three more outs. After retiring Goslin and Manush, the Cuban righthander yielded a single to Cronin and a walk to Schulte. Then he struck out Kuhel to end the game and send the Giants to the world championship.

Ott's dramatic home run had made the difference. The little guy with the funny swing had hit the most crucial home run of his career. Mel finished the Series with a .389 batting average with seven hits in 18 trips to the plate. The Giants, however, would not win another fall classic until 1954.

Ott continued his excellent career until 1947. By then, he had become manager of the Giants, too, taking the job in 1942 at the age of 32. He served in the post until midway through the 1948 season.

When he retired as a player, Ott had hit more home runs than any National League batter. And he remains to this day the smallest slugger ever to hit 500 or more homers. None, though. was any bigger than the 10th-inning blow that won the 1933 World Series.

New York	AB	R	H	RBI	Washington	AB	R	H	RBI
Moore, lf	5	0	1	0	Myer, 2b	5	0	0	0
Critz, 2b	5	0	0	0	Goslin, rf	4	0	1	0
Terry, 1b	5	0	2	0	Manush, lf	5	1	1	0
Ott, rf	5	1	1	1	Cronin, ss	5	1	3	0
Davis, cf	5	1	2	0	Schulte, cf	4	1	2	3
Jackson, 3b	3	1	1	0	Kerr-pr	0	0	0	0
Mancuso, c	3	1	1	1	Kuhel, 1b	5	0	2	0
Ryan, ss	2	0	1	0	Bluege, 2b	4	0	1	0
Schumacher, p	3	0	1	2	Sewell, c	4	0	0	0
Luque, p	1	0	1	0	Crowder, p	2	0	0	0
					Russell, p	1	0	0	0
Totals	37	4	11	4		39	3	10	3

	1	2	3	4	5	6	7	8	9	10	
New York	0	2	0	0	0	1	0	0	0	1	**4**
Washington	0	0	0	0	0	3	0	0	0	0	**3**

New York	IP	H	R	ER	BB	SO
Schumacher	5⅔	8	3	3	1	1
Luque (W)	4⅓	2	0	0	2	5
Washington	**IP**	**H**	**R**	**ER**	**BB**	**SO**
Crowder	5⅓	7	3	3	2	4
Russell (L)	4⅔	4	1	1	0	3

E–Jackson. DP–New York 1, Washington 1. LOB–New York 7, Washington 9. 2B–Davis, Mancuso. HR–Schulte, Ott. SH–Ryan, Jackson. WP–Crowder, Schumacher. T–2:38. A–28,454.

Gabby Hartnett

The Homer in the Gloamin'

September 28, 1938 Wrigley Field

One of the advantages of being a playing-manager was that it sometimes provided the opportunity to lead by example. There was never a better demonstration of how well that could work than the one performed by Charles (Gabby) Hartnett on a dreary fall afternoon in Chicago.

There is, of course, no such thing as a playing-manager anymore. That once-familiar title has vanished even more thoroughly than nine-inning pitchers and adept bunters. But Hartnett was one of many in his era who filled that role, and one day he gave the boys a lesson in how to win a pennant.

On September 28, 1938, with darkness closing in, Hartnett socked a home run in the bottom of the ninth inning to give the Chicago Cubs a 6–5 victory over the Pittsburgh Pirates. The blow nudged the Cubs into first place ahead of the Bucs, and three days later a pennant flew in Chicago.

There was actually a time when the word "pennant" was familiar to Cubs fans. Unlike the last 50-plus barren years, the Bruins won National League flags with some regularity. They won in 1929, 1932, and 1935. They would win yet again—for the last time—in 1945. And although all five pennants resulted in World Series losses, at least the Cubs of that era got a chance to smell the roses.

Hartnett had become Chicago's manager midway through the 1938 season when he replaced Charlie Grimm. The Cubs were stuck in a swamp of mediocrity under Grimm, and when Jolly Cholly could get no better than a 45–36 record out of them, he was dumped in favor of the hard-hitting catcher.

A native of Woonsocket, Rhode Island, the moon-faced backstop with no managerial experience had been with the Cubs since 1922. He was a solid player who not only hit for high average and power, but was an excellent receiver with a rifle arm.

Gabby, who got his nickname as a boy who rarely talked, had had some outstanding seasons, most notably in 1930 when he hit .339 with 37 home runs and 122 RBI. An effusive talker once he reached the big leagues, he batted .344 in 1935 and .354 in 1937.

Home runs were a familiar commodity with Hartnett. He homered in double figures in 12 of his 20 big league seasons, and along with a lifetime batting average of .297 finished his career with the highest number of four-baggers (236) of any catcher who played the game up to that time.

When Harnett, the acknowledged leader of the Cubs, was given the managerial reigns, he was taking over a team that had been floundering badly. Despite a strong club that featured Stan Hack, Augie Galan, Billy Herman, Hartnett, and slick-fielding Bill Jurges, the Cubs at one point under Grimm had lost 11 of 12 games and were on the verge of fading out of the pennant race.

Hartnett assumed command on July 20 with the Cubs in third place, 5½ games behind the Pirates. Pittsburgh won 40 of 54 games in June and July. But slowly, under the aggressive leadership of the new skipper, Chicago began to improve. Although the club fell to seven games back by the beginning of September, it had moved up to second place and was winning steadily.

The Pirates, meanwhile, cruised along, fully expecting to capture the pennant. So confident was Pittsburgh that the club ordered World Series tickets printed and began making alterations to Forbes Field.

But by the evening of September 26, the Cubs had whittled the lead down to 1½ games. And the stage was set for a showdown with the Pirates, who were coming to Wrigley Field for a three-game series.

Gabby Hartnett was welcomed by his Cubs teammates as he crossed the plate in semidarkness.

"We've got to take this series," Pirates manager Pie Traynor intoned. "Chicago's pitchers will be pitching with insufficient rest, but my pitchers are ready."

Hartnett summoned sore-armed Dizzy Dean, the former St. Louis Cardinals great whom the Cubs had acquired in a trade before the 1938 season after he was injured in the All-Star Game the previous year. Dean responded by pitching eight shutout innings and leading the Cubs to a 2–1 victory. The Cubs were now just one-half game out of first.

The following afternoon 34,465 highly vocal fans packed Wrigley Field to watch Cubs 19-game winner Clay Bryant square off against Pirates rookie Bob Klinger, winner of 12 games. It was a cloudy day, not particularly suitable for a baseball game.

Chicago scored an unearned run in the second after Jurges reached first with two outs when Pirate catcher Al Todd missed the third strike, then Lee Handley scooped up Bryant's grounder and threw it into the stands, allowing Rip Collins to score. Handley redeemed himself with a two-run single that sparked a three-run Pittsburgh sixth, but the Cubs bounced back to tie the score with two runs in the bottom of the sixth on doubles by Hartnett and Collins, a bunt, and an infield out.

The 3–3 tie stood until the eighth, when the Bucs tallied twice on run-scoring singles by Manusch and Handley. But the Cubs came back with a pair of runs in the bottom half on an RBI double by pinch hitter Tony Lazzeri and Billy Herman's bases-loaded hit. At the conclusion of the inning, with the score tied at 5–5, umpires notified each team that no further inning would be played after the ninth. If a tie existed, the game would be replayed in its entirety as part of a doubleheader the next day.

Charlie Root, the sixth Cubs pitcher, retired the Pirates in the top of the inning. But it was getting darker by the minute. As the Cubs came to bat, it was becoming hard to see the outfielders.

Mace Brown, who had entered the game in the eighth and gotten the Pirates out of a jam with an inning-ending doubleplay, was on the mound as the bottom of the ninth began. He quickly set down Phil Cavarretta on a fly into the darkness that somehow Lloyd Waner caught in center field and Carl Reynolds on a bouncer to second.

Then up stepped Hartnett. Brown fired two quick curves for strikes. On the third pitch, Brown came back with another curve. Hartnett swung, and while nearly everyone in the park strained to see where it was headed, the ball traveled to deep left and disappeared into the stands.

Hartnett peered into the darkness, then started running. He knew he had just given his team a 6–5 victory. Ironically, the win went to Charlie Root, the same pitcher who had yielded Babe Ruth's "called shot" in the 1932 World Series.

"A lot of people told me they didn't know the ball was in the bleachers," Gabby said many years later. "Well, I did. Maybe I was the only one in the park who did. But I knew it the moment I hit it."

So apparently did Brown. At the crack of the bat, he put his head down and without watching the flight of the ball, headed for the Pittsburgh clubhouse.

Cubs fans poured out of the stands and joined Hartnett in his triumphant journey around the bases. As Hartnett battled to touch the bases, some fans picked him up as he rounded second and again when he reached third. Ushers ran ahead of Gabby trying to clear a path. Fists flew as a frenzied mob battled the ushers to reach the new hero.

Finally, Hartnett battled his way to the plate, barely managing to escape the grasp of the fans to touch it as umpire George Barr stood stoically to one side, making sure the final base was touched.

As fans continued to swarm around him, ushers, police, and a few players, fearing for Hartnett's life, fought their way back into the crowd to rescue the Cubs manager and carry him to the safety of the clubhouse.

"Brown pumped with everything he had, and I swung with every ounce of strength I possessed," Hartnett said later.

Sportswriters, always quick to pounce on a good idea, borrowed from the Scottish word for dusk and quickly named the feat "The Homer in the Gloamin'." The name stuck, and forever after, that's what Hartnett's homer would be called.

The Cubs now had a one-half game lead. They still had to meet the Pirates again, but the demoralized Bucs had nothing left. Chicago blew them away, 10–1. The Chicago lead was up to 1½ games, but two games remained in the season. A tie game with the Cardinals was called after nine innings because of darkness while Pittsburgh split a doubleheader in Cincinnati. Then, while the Pirates were losing to the Reds on the last day of the season, Chicago divided a twin bill with St. Louis.

Winning 21 of their last 25 games, the Cubs finished the season with an 89–63 record and a two-game lead over the Pirates. Hartnett, whose mark was 44–27 after becoming manager, led the Cubs into a World Series in which they lost four straight to the New York Yankees.

Hartnett was let go as Cubs manager after the 1940 season. He played in 1941 with the New York Giants, then retired. In 1955, he was elected to the Hall of Fame. Nothing he did to get him there quite compared, however, to the mighty home run he slammed through the darkness in that famous game in 1938.

Pittsburgh	AB	R	H	RBI	Chicago	AB	R	H	RBI
L. Waner, cf	4	0	2	0	Hack, 3b	3	0	0	1
P. Waner, rf	5	0	2	0	Herman, 2b	5	0	3	1
Rizzo, lf	4	1	1	1	Demaree, lf	5	0	0	0
Vaughan, ss	2	2	1	0	Cavarretta, rf	5	0	0	0
Suhr, 1b	3	2	1	0	Reynolds, cf	5	0	1	0
Young, 2b	2	0	0	0	Hartnett, c	4	2	2	1
Manush, ph	1	0	1	1	Collins, 1b	4	3	3	1
Thevenow, 2b	0	0	0	0	Jurges, ss	3	1	1	0
Handley, 3b	4	0	2	3	Bryant, p	2	0	1	0
Todd, c	4	0	0	0	Russell, p	0	0	0	0
Klinger, p	4	0	0	0	O'Dea, ph	1	0	0	0
Swift, p	0	0	0	0	Page, p	0	0	0	0
Brown, p	0	0	0	0	French, p	0	0	0	0
					Lee, p	0	0	0	0
					Lazzeri, ph	1	0	1	1
					Marty, pr	0	0	0	0
					Root, p	0	0	0	0
Totals	33	5	10	5		38	6	12	5

Pittsburgh	0	0	0	0	0	3	0	2	0	**5**
Chicago	0	1	0	0	0	2	0	2	1	**6**

Two outs when winning run scored

Pittsburgh	IP	H	R	ER	BB	SO
Klinger	7	9	4	3	2	6
Swift	⅓	2	1	1	2	0
Brown (L)	1⅓	1	1	1	0	0

Chicago	IP	H	R	ER	BB	SO
Bryant	5⅔	4	3	3	5	1
Russell	⅓	0	0	0	0	0
Page	1	3	2	2	1	1
French	0	1	0	0	0	0
Lee	1	1	0	0	0	0
Root (W)	1	1	0	0	0	0

E–P. Waner, Vaughan, Handley, Todd. DP–Pittsburgh 1, Chicago 3. LOB–Pittsburgh 7, Chicago 10. 2B–L. Waner, Hartnett, Collins, Lazzeri. HR–Hartnett. WP–Lee. T–2:37. A–34,465.

Whitey Kurowski

The End of a Remarkable Season

October 5, 1942 Yankee Stadium

One of the many endearing qualities of the game of baseball is its unpredictability. There is no such thing as a sure thing.

George (Whitey) Kurowski could certainly attest to that fact. He was a guy who began his rookie season on the bench and ended it by winning a World Series at the conclusion of one of the most thrilling, as well as extraordinary, seasons ever played.

The year was 1942. It was not a good year for the world, but it was a glittering year for baseball, in particular the St. Louis Cardinals.

With the disaster at Pearl Harbor having taken place just a few months earlier on December 7, 1941, and the United States just beginning to emerge from the ravages of the Great Depression and now plunging into a worldwide war, it was a somber time throughout the country. Baseball, which vowed to remain in operation despite the increasing loss of players to the military draft, was one of the few pleasant diversions still available.

No one could predict it at the time, but the 1942 season would be the last one until World War II ended in which baseball was at full strength. The next three seasons would see the quality of the game deteriorate to a substantially lower level as numerous players marched off to war and were replaced by a collection of players who were not of major league caliber.

The '42 campaign was also noteworthy for another reason. It was a marvelous season all around, and in the National League, the Cardinals and Brooklyn Dodgers engaged in one of the greatest pennant races of all time.

As defending National League champions, the Dodgers were heavily favored to win the flag again. And they gave no reason to believe otherwise as they exploded out of the gate and quickly mounted a big early lead.

The Cardinals played just .500 ball in the early going, and by early May were already 7½ games out of first. Finally, on May 25, with the team still struggling, St. Louis manager Billy Southworth made a crucial decision. He inserted rookie George Kurowski into the lineup at third base while moving veteran Jimmy Brown to second and sending Frank (Creepy) Crespi to the bench.

Kurowski, a 24-year-old blond who had been in the Cardinals' farm system since 1937, had batted just nine times in a late-season call-up the year before. Along with a fine minor league record, he also carried with him an unusual physical disability. His right arm was three to four inches shorter than his left arm, the result of a boyhood fall from a fence. The injury had given him a blood infection that turned into osteomyelitis and required surgery in which part of the ulna had to be removed.

The injury never affected the righthanded Kurowski's playing ability, although professional teams had been reluctant to take a chance on him until the Cardinals signed him. It turned into a fortuitous move for the Redbirds, especially after Southworth made Whitey his third baseman as the team began a series with the Chicago Cubs.

In his first start, Kurowski got two hits in a 10–2 Cards victory. That began a hot streak that carried St. Louis into second place. Through midsummer, however, the Cardinals still hadn't been able to catch the Dodgers. By August 15, they trailed Brooklyn by 10 games, despite a splendid 63–40 record. But after winning three of four games in a late-August series with Brooklyn, the Cards had narrowed the margin to 5½ games.

"Don't worry about us," feisty Dodgers manager Leo Durocher chanted. "It might be a little harder than we anticipated. But we'll win the pennant again."

By September 11, however, the Brooklyn lead had shrunk to two

The mighty Yankees fell with one swing of **Whitey Kurowski's** powerful bat.

games as the teams met in a crucial series at Ebbets Field. St. Louis won both games, with Kurowski's two-run homer giving the Cards a 2–1 win in the second game.

St. Louis went into the lead the next day with a victory over the Philadelphia Phillies. The Cards stayed in first the rest of the season, climaxing a blistering stretch drive by winning 21 of 25 games in September and 41 of their final 48 games to finish with a club record 106 wins. The Dodgers, two games back, won 20 of their last 25 games to finish with 104 wins, the most for a runner-up team since 1909.

With 22-game winner and National League Most Valuable Player Mort Cooper and rookie 21-game winner Johnny Beazley leading the way, the Cardinals pitching staff posted a league-leading 2.55 earned run average, the lowest in the major leagues since 1919.

For the Cardinals, it was their sixth pennant, but first since 1934. And it would launch them on a streak of three straight flags and four NL titles in five years.

In the World Series, the Cardinals, a team made up mostly of young players who had come up through the club's farm system—including another rookie named Stan Musial, as well as star players such as right fielder Enos Slaughter, center fielder Terry Moore, shortstop Marty Marion, first baseman Johnny Hopp, and catcher Walker Cooper—seemed to be no match for the powerful New York Yankees. A veteran squad that had won six World Series in the last seven years, the Yanks had won 103 games themselves in 1942, storming home with the flag nine games ahead of the second-place Boston Red Sox.

New York had an awesome lineup that featured future Hall of Famers Joe DiMaggio, Bill Dickey, and Phil Rizzuto, plus heavy hitters Charley Keller, Tommy Henrich, and Joe Gordon, the American League's Most Valuable Player that year. They also had a formidable pitching staff led by 21-game winner Ernie Bonham.

The Yanks were heavily favored to win the Series. But the Cardinals showed no signs of being intimidated. "We won [the pennant] on our own power, and we'll do the same against the Yankees," said Southworth. "We can give the Yankees the best we have, and we think that will be enough."

The Cards then went out and lost the first game, 7–4, as Yankees starter Red Ruffing struck out Kurowski three times. Beazley beat Bonham in a brilliant matchup of 21-game winners in the second game, 4–3, and Ernie White pitched a six-hitter and Kurowski scored the game's only run in a 1–0 Cardinals victory in Game 3. Kurowski's two-run single helped the Cards to a 9–6 victory in the fourth game as Max Lanier got the win in relief of Cooper.

That set the stage for Game 5 at Yankee Stadium. Beazley, who would soon enter military service and never again come close to his spectacular '42 season, got the start for the Cardinals against Ruffing, a future Hall of Famer. "I'll be damned if I intend to go back to St. Louis and play more baseball," Beazley had said.

Some 69,052 jammed the stands for what would be a high-pressure battle. Light-hitting Rizzuto hit a leadoff homer for the Yanks in the first, but Enos Slaughter answered with a four-bagger for the Cards in the fourth. DiMaggio's RBI single in the fourth and Walker Cooper's sacrifice fly in the sixth kept the game tied at 2–2.

No more runs scored, and the tension mounted as the Cardinals came to bat in the top of the ninth. Walker Cooper led off the inning with a single. He moved to second on Hopp's sacrifice bunt. Kurowski was next.

Whitey had hit just .254 during the regular season with nine home runs. He had three hits in 14 at-bats so far in the Series. Along with being blanked by Ruffing in the first game, he had no hits in three at-bats against the Yankees righthander in Game 5.

But this time it was different. Kurowski turned on a Ruffing pitch and lashed a drive down the left-field line that carried into the bleachers, giving Whitey a two-run homer and the Cardinals a 4–2 lead.

"He threw me a good pitch," Kurowski said years later. "It was a high, inside fastball. I got around on it. I was just hoping it would stay fair. It was just inside the left-field foul line.

"It was getting dark at the time," Kurowski added. "We were a little concerned about that. But mainly, we just wanted to get them out in the ninth and go home."

It was up to Beazley to retire the Yankees in the bottom of the ninth. He did, but with a special assist from Walker Cooper. With two on and none out, the Cards catcher picked off Gordon at second base to help quell a Yankees uprising.

A few minutes later, the Cardinals were in the clubhouse celebrating a World Series victory. "It was pretty calm," Kurowoski remembered. "We did a little celebrating, but not much. We didn't celebrate then like they do today.

"For me, it was the most memorable hit of my career because it helped—and I emphasize helped—to win a World Series. It always takes nine to win a ball game, and I was just one of them. But it was a great feeling getting that home run because we were such underdogs in the Series."

Whitey, who for many years carried the stub from his first big league paycheck in his wallet (showing he made $226.61 for two weeks work), went on to a fine career in the big leagues, hitting .286 with 106 home runs before retiring in 1949. But there was nothing that quite compared with the home run he hit in 1942 to win a World Series.

St. Louis	AB	R	H	RBI	New York	AB	R	H	RBI
Brown, 2b	3	0	2	0	Rizzuto, ss	4	1	2	1
Moore, cf	3	1	1	0	Rolfe, 3b	4	1	1	0
Slaughter, rf	4	1	2	1	Cullenbine, rf	4	0	0	0
Musial, lf	4	0	0	0	DiMaggio, cf	4	0	1	1
W. Cooper, c	4	1	2	1	Keller, lf	4	0	1	0
Hopp, 1b	3	0	0	0	Gordon, 2b	4	0	1	0
Kurowski, 3b	4	1	1	2	Dickey, c	4	0	0	0
Marion, ss	4	0	0	0	Stainback, pr	0	0	0	0
Beazley, p	4	0	1	0	Priddy, 1b	3	0	0	0
					Ruffing, p	3	0	1	0
					Selkirk, ph	1	0	0	0
Totals	33	4	9	4		35	2	7	2

St. Louis	0 0 0 1 0 1 0 0 2 **4**
New York	1 0 0 1 0 0 0 0 0 **2**

St. Louis	IP	H	R	ER	BB	SO
Beazley (W)	9	7	2	2	1	2
New York	**IP**	**H**	**R**	**ER**	**BB**	**SO**
Ruffing (L)	9	9	4	4	1	3

E—Brown 2, Hopp, Beazley, Priddy. DP—St. Louis 1, New York 1. LOB—St. Louis 5, New York 7. HR—Rizzuto, Slaughter, Kurowski. SH—Moore, Hopp. T—1:58. A—69,052.

Hank Greenberg

A Triumphant Return from the War

September 30, 1945 Sportsman's Park

The game of baseball is filled with examples of players who made remarkable comebacks. Some did it after overcoming serious injuries; others did it following significant slippages in their performances.

And then there was Hank Greenberg. He, like very few others, did it after being away from the game for more than four years.

Not only did Greenberg make a spectacular comeback after serving in the military service during World War II, but just under four months after he returned to the lineup, the big left fielder also slugged a memorable ninth-inning, grand-slam home run that won a pennant for the Detroit Tigers.

It came on September 30, 1945, in what turned out to be the last game of the season. It was the biggest homer in Tigers history, and it brought a flag to the Motor City for the first time in five years.

Few players picked up where they left off after returning to the major leagues from military service in World War II. It took most of them—if they made it back at all—a long time to shed the rust of having no baseball activity and to overcome the detrimental effects of having fought in a war.

These effects, however, were minimal for Greenberg, a future Hall of

Famer. He made his comeback with a flourish. When he returned to the lineup, it was almost as though he had never been away.

Greenberg had been the first major league player inducted into military service when he was drafted into the army on May 7, 1941. Because he was 30 years old at the time—and military regulations allowed for draftees over 28 to be released—Big Henry was sent home on December 5, 1941. Two days later, Pearl Harbor was bombed, and Greenberg immediately reenlisted into the army air force.

"We are in trouble, and there's only one thing for me to do," he said. "Return to the service. I have not been called back. I am going back on my own accord, and baseball is out the window as far as I'm concerned. I don't know if I'll ever return."

Greenberg left behind a glittering career. A two-time Most Valuable Player (1935, 1940), he was one of the premier hitters in baseball. A big, strong, 6–4, 215-pound righthanded swinger, he had come off the streets of New York City to sign with the Tigers in 1930 and would soon become the first great Jewish major league player.

Since joining the Tigers in 1933, Greenberg had led or tied for three home run crowns, including in 1938 when he chased Babe Ruth's record before ending the season with 58 four-baggers. He had driven in 170 runs in 1935 and 183 in 1937, and while hitting above .300 every year had led Detroit to three pennants and one World Series victory.

When Greenberg's departure from baseball interrupted a brilliant eight-year stretch of accomplishments, he'd appeared in just 19 games in 1941. He would not set foot on a baseball diamond again until 1945.

Hank entered the army as a private and came out as a captain. During his tour of duty, he served much of his time in Asia. Greenberg was 34 years old when he was finally discharged on June 14, 1945, as the war was winding down.

Soon afterward, Hank reported to the Tigers. He was rusty and out of shape, and few thought he could ever make it back to the playing field after not swinging a bat for more than four years. But Greenberg worked out diligently, and on June 21 he rejoined the Tigers. Then on July 1, manager Steve O'Neill penciled Hank's name in the starting lineup in left field. "We need some long hits," the skipper said, "and Hank is the boy who will deliver them."

Playing before a Briggs Stadium crowd of 55,000, Greenberg hit an eighth-inning home run to help beat the Philadelphia Athletics, 9–5, in the first game of a doubleheader. It was a moment he had dreamed about all those lonely nights in distant places in Asia.

Hank, however, had no time to squander on idle thoughts. Detroit was embroiled in a fierce pennant race with the surprising Washington Senators. The Senators had finished in eighth place the year before, and no one expected them to be a contender, least of all Washington owner Clark Griffith.

Thinking his team wouldn't be in the race, Griffith had leased the team's Griffith Stadium to the NFL Washington Redskins for the final week of the baseball season. The Senators would end their season one week early by piling up doubleheaders.

On June 12, the move seemed logical. Washington roosted in seventh place. But within one month, the Nats had climbed to second, 4½ games behind the Tigers. The Senators stayed hot, while the Tigers faltered, and by the time the two teams met in a five-game series in Washington in mid-September, only one-half game separated them. After winning three of the five games, Detroit left town clinging to a 1½ game lead.

When their season ended on September 23, Washington had an 87–67 record, trailing the Tigers by one game. But while Washington sat, Detroit split a doubleheader with the Cleveland Indians, then had three off days before going to St. Louis for a two-game series with the third-place Browns, the defending American League champions, on the final weekend of the season. When Saturday's game was rained out, a doubleheader was scheduled for Sunday with the Tigers still holding a one-game lead.

Detroit had to win one game to clinch the pennant. O'Neill made a surprise selection for the first game, sending Virgil Trucks to the mound. Trucks was an outstanding pitcher, but he had just been discharged from military service three days earlier after spending nearly two years on active duty.

Trucks, however, declared himself fit and ready to go, a welcome sign for O'Neill's tired and overworked pitching staff. His opponent was 34-year-old Nelson Potter, a 15-game winner who had tossed a two-hit shutout against the Tigers just two weeks earlier.

It had rained all day, and the start of the game was delayed 50 minutes as members of the ground crew tried to chase away the water with mops and brooms. Only 5,532 fans were in the stands.

Although Trucks was sharp at the beginning, he gave up one run in the first. Detroit retaliated with single runs in the fifth and sixth, taking the lead on an RBI single by Paul Richards. Then in the sixth, the Browns seemed on the verge of blowing the game open.

Tiring rapidly, Trucks gave up a one-out double to Potter and a walk to Don Gutteridge. Trucks was then replaced by the Tigers ace, Hal Newhouser. After walking Lou Finney to load the bases, Newhouser escaped the jam by striking out Mark Christman and retiring George McQuinn as Doc Cramer made a fine running catch of a line drive in right-center.

The Browns tied the score in the seventh on Vern Stephens's RBI single, then went ahead in the eighth as one-armed Pete Gray raced home from first on a double by McQuinn. All the while, rain continued to fall, and darkness was closing in, making the second game virtually impossible.

Detroit had one more chance in the ninth. Pinch-hitter Hub Walker, batting for Newhouser, led off with a single, and was safe at second on a controversial call when the Browns tried to get him on Skeeter Webb's bunt attempt. Eddie Mayo then sacrificed the runners up before Cramer was walked intentionally to load the bases.

Greenberg was next. Hank, who had hit 12 home runs, had driven in 56, and was batting a lofty .309 in his half season of play, had cost the Tigers a possible run earlier in the game when he was picked off third base. Now, he was at bat with the Browns hoping he would hit into a doubleplay.

The Senators were all listening on the radio back in Washington. They had already sent their top pitcher, Dutch Leonard, to Detroit to rest and prepare for a playoff game.

Hank took the first pitch for a ball. The second pitch was over the plate, and Greenberg swung. A low rocket flew off his bat, traveled down the left-field line, and landed in the stands just a few feet inside the foul pole for a grand-slam home run.

"As Potter wound up, I could read his grip on the ball," Hank said later, "and I could tell he was going to throw a screwball. After I swung, I stood at the plate and watched for fear the umpire would call it foul."

He didn't, and the blow delivered a 6–3 lead to the Tigers.

As he trotted around the bases, Greenberg thought back to his war days overseas. "It was the strangest thing," he said. "I wasn't sure if I was awake or dreaming."

With darkness closing in, Al Benton retired the Browns in the bottom

Hank Greenberg (*right*) got a hug from winning pitcher Virgil (Fire) Trucks after his grand slam brought the Tigers a pennant.

of the ninth, and Detroit danced off the field with the pennant. The second game was canceled because of rain. Newhouser was credited with his 25th win, and the Tigers ended the season with an 88–65 record, good for a 1½-game lead over the Senators. (Teams in those days were not required to make up unplayed games, even if they affected the pennant race.)

Detroit went on to defeat the Chicago Cubs in seven games of the World Series with Greenberg contributing two more home runs, including a three-run shot that gave Trucks a 4–1 win in the second game.

The homer that beat the Browns turned out to be the last grand slam in Greenberg's career. Hank went on to play just two more years, winning one final home run title in 1946 before finishing his career the following season with the Pittsburgh Pirates. Of his 331 career homers, the one that stood out the most was his sizzling blast that capped a triumphant return in 1945.

Detroit	**AB**	**R**	**H**	**RBI**	**St. Louis**	**AB**	**R**	**H**	**RBI**
Webb, ss	5	1	1	0	Gutteridge, 2b	3	1	1	0
Mayo, 2b	4	0	1	1	Finney, lf	3	0	2	1
Cramer, cf	5	1	1	0	Byrnes, cf	3	0	0	0
Greenberg, lf	5	1	2	4	Christman, ph	1	0	0	0
Cullenbine, rf	4	1	1	0	Gray, cf	1	1	0	0
York, 1b	5	0	0	0	McQuinn, 1b	4	0	1	1
Outlaw, 3b	3	0	1	0	Moore, rf	4	1	1	0
Richards, c	4	0	1	1	Stephens, ss	4	0	2	1
Trucks, p	2	1	0	0	Mancuso, c	4	0	0	0
Newhouser, p	0	0	0	0	Schulte, 3b	4	0	0	0
Walker, ph	1	0	1	0	Potter, p	3	0	1	0
Boron, pr	0	1	0	0					
Benton, p	0	0	0	0					
Totals	38	6	9	6		34	3	8	3

Detroit	0	0	0	0	1	1	0	0	4	**6**
St. Louis	1	0	0	0	0	0	1	1	0	**3**

Detroit	IP	H	R	ER	BB	SO
Trucks	5⅓	3	1	1	3	3
Newhouser (W)	2⅔	4	2	2	1	5
Benton	1	1	0	0	0	0
St. Louis	**IP**	**H**	**R**	**ER**	**BB**	**SO**
Potter (L)	9	9	6	6	5	4

2B–Gutteridge, Potter, McQuinn, Moore. HR–Greenberg. SF–Webb, Mayo. DP–Detroit 2. LOB–Detroit 8, St. Louis 5. T–2:32. A–5,532.

Dick Sisler

Bats Phillies to First Flag in 35 Years

October 1, 1950 Ebbets Field

In the long and mostly undistinguished life of the Philadelphia Phillies, thousands of home runs have been hit by the more than 1,600 players who have worn the uniform of the team. None, however, was more memorable, more dramatic, or more significant than the one hit by Dick Sisler.

Coming against the Brooklyn Dodgers on the final day of the 1950 season, it gave the Phillies their first National League pennant in 35 years and their only flag between 1915 and 1980.

Sisler's blast—with two men on base—broke a 1–1 tie in the 10th inning and sent the Phillies home with a 4–1 victory. The hit climaxed a long and arduous season for the Phillies and produced one of the most joyous celebrations ever staged in the city of Philadelphia.

Sisler was a somewhat unlikely hero, although he was one of the club's most popular players. On a team that was built around young players such as future Hall of Famers Robin Roberts and Richie Ashburn, slugger Del Ennis, and fiery team captain Granny Hamner, he was not one of the Phillies' marquee names. At 29 years old in 1950, Dick was somewhat older than most of the youthful Phils, although veterans such as 1950 MVP Jim Konstanty and Andy Seminick were major components of the team.

Sisler had joined the Phillies in 1948 after arriving in a trade with the St. Louis Cardinals, the team with which he entered the majors in 1946. He was the regular first baseman in his first year with the Phillies, but was ticketed for reserve duty in 1949 after the club acquired first baseman Eddie Waitkus from the Chicago Cubs. But when Waitkus was shot by a deranged, 19-year-old woman in a Chicago hotel room in June, Sisler regained his job at first base, and wound up the season with a respectable .280 batting average.

Dick was not known as a home run hitter. In his entire eight-year career, the 6–2, 205-pound lefthanded batter hit only 55 home runs to go along with his .276 lifetime batting average. He never hit more than 13 homers in a season.

"If I hadn't [hit the home run], I don't think people would have remembered me," Sisler said. "I was just another ball player, maybe a little bit better than average."

But Sisler, a St. Louis, Missouri, native whose brother Dave pitched in the big leagues, was more than up to the task on that storied October 1 afternoon at Ebbets Field. It's a good thing he was because the Phillies, whose history over the previous 32 years was filled with pathetic losers and only two first division finishes, were on the verge of blowing what would be their biggest chance to win a pennant since they finished second in 1917.

Regarded as a team on the rise after their third-place finish in 1949, the Phillies were not expected to be one of the main contenders in 1950. But the Phils, who that year because of their youth had been nicknamed the Whiz Kids, surprised everybody by getting off to a fast start. The club bounced in and out of first place in the early months before surging to a permanent hold on the league lead in late July. By the end of August, they led by as much as nine and one-half games.

A devastating September slump, however, sent the Phillies reeling. Even with 11 games left to play, though, they still held a seven-game lead. But the losses continued to mount, reducing the Phillies lead to a mere two games as the team entered the last weekend of the season with a two-game series against the red-hot Dodgers. Brooklyn had won 12 of its last 15 games. Two wins against the Phillies would create a tie, forcing a play-off between the two teams.

The Phillies, under manager Eddie Sawyer, were exhausted and riddled with injuries to key players. A playoff meant almost certain defeat. The Phils absolutely had to win one of the two games. When they lost the first one, 7–3, the stage was set for a tense showdown on the last day.

The meeting was packed with irony. The Dodgers were managed by Burt Shotton, a former Phillies skipper who in 1932 had led the team to fourth place, its highest finish between 1918 and 1948. Working for the Dodgers as chief scout and top assistant to general manager Branch Rickey was George Sisler, a member of the Hall of Fame and Dick's father. Brooklyn's third base coach, Milt Stock, was the Phillies third baseman the last time the club won a pennant in 1915.

Brooklyn was a powerhouse club that was in the midst of a glorious era. Between 1946 and 1956 the team won six pennants and three times lost flags on the last day of the season. Fielding a lineup with future Hall of Famers Jackie Robinson, Pee Wee Reese, Roy Campanella, and Duke Snider, plus a supporting cast that included Carl Furillo and Gil Hodges, the Dodgers had one of the great teams of all time.

With several thousand Phillies fans making the trip to Brooklyn to root for their team and a crowd of 35,073 jammed into tiny Ebbets Field—an estimated 30,000 more were turned away at the gate—Roberts, pitching on just two days' rest, took the mound for the Whiz Kids against Don Newcombe. Each was going for his 20th win of the season.

The two mound titans piched magnificently. The Phillies grabbed a 1–0 lead in the top of the sixth when Sisler singled and, after another single by Ennis, scampered home on a single by Willie Jones. Brooklyn came right back to tie the bottom half of the inning when Reese hit a ball that lodged at the base of a wire screen in right-center field and he trotted around the bases with a controversial ground-rule home run.

The 1–1 score was still standing in the bottom of the ninth. Cal Abrams led off for the Dodgers with a walk and moved to second on a single by Reese. Snider then drilled a liner to center. Ashburn, playing shallow, fielded the ball on one hop and fired it to the plate as Abrams was unwisely waved home by Dodgers third base coach Stock. Catcher Stan Lopata tagged out Abrams 15 feet up the line.

With what would have been the winning run cut down, Roberts issued an intentional walk to Robinson to load the bases before retiring Furillo and Hodges to end the ninth and send the game into extra innings.

The weary Roberts led off the 10th with a single. Waitkus followed with another single. Then Ashburn tried to sacrifice, but Roberts was thrown out at third, getting a painful dose of lime in his eye as he slid.

Next up was Sisler, who already had three singles in the game, despite a heavily taped and badly sprained wrist that had kept him out of action three weeks earlier and that he had aggravated sliding into second in the fourth inning. Sisler, however, usually fared well against Newcombe, and would hit .329 against him in 1950.

The fireballing Newcombe got two quick strikes, then wasted a ball. Then he threw one he would regret forever.

"It was a fastball over the plate, high and away," Sisler recalled. "I swung hard, just hoping I could make contact. The ball sailed out to left field. I didn't think it would go out, so I began running. As I rounded first, I saw it was a home run."

From the upper porch of his home in suburban Philadelphia, **Dick Sisler** greeted Phillies fans gathered in the street the morning after his home run.

The ball cleared the left-field wall with plenty of room to spare. As his father George watched with mixed emotions from the stands, finally happily tossing his hat in the air, Sisler romped quickly around the bases, arriving at the plate to be engulfed by a mob of ecstatic Whiz Kids.

"As I circled the bases, I thought that would be enough for Roberts because he was tough that day," Sisler said. "He was dead tired, but he was able to dig down and come up with a little extra."

Roberts, pitching the grittiest performance of his life, retired the Dodgers in order in the bottom of the 10th. And the Phillies had only the second pennant in club history.

"I've hit some better, but none ever meant so much," said Sisler amid the pandemonium of the Phillies locker room. "It's the biggest hit I ever got."

As soon as the game ended, the celebration began back in Philadelphia. Jubilant Phillies fans spilled into the streets. Car horns honked. Church bells rang. Fire sirens blared. Impromptu parades began as Philadelphians launched a wild party that extended far into the night.

When the Phillies' train arrived in Philadelphia a few hours after the end of the game, thousands of fans mobbed the station, hoping to get a glimpse of the players.

The euphoria, however, was short-lived. The Phillies lost four straight games to the New York Yankees in the World Series, then soon sank back into the lower levels of the National League standings. No National League pennant would fly in Philadelphia for another 30 years.

Back in Brooklyn, the Dodgers fired Shotton and Stock. As for Sisler, who ended the season with a .296 batting average, he was traded after the 1951 campaign. But his name had become a household word in Philadelphia, and he would forever be remembered as the man who slammed the biggest hit in Phillies history.

Philadelphia	AB	R	H	RBI	Brooklyn	AB	R	H	RBI
Waitkus, 1b	5	1	1	0	Abrams, lf	2	0	0	0
Ashburn, cf	5	1	0	0	Reese, ss	4	1	3	1
Sisler, lf	5	2	4	3	Snider, cf	4	0	1	0
Mayo, lf	0	0	0	0	Robinson, 2b	3	0	0	0
Ennis, rf	5	0	2	0	Furillo, rf	4	0	0	0
Jones, 3b	5	0	1	1	Hodges, 1b	4	0	0	0
Hamner, ss	4	0	0	0	Campanella, c	4	0	1	0
Seminick, c	3	0	1	0	Cox, 3b	3	0	0	0
Caballero, pr	0	0	0	0	Russell, ph	1	0	0	0
Lopata, c	0	0	0	0	Newcombe, p	3	0	0	0
Goliat, 2b	4	0	1	0	Brown, ph	1	0	0	0
Roberts, p	2	0	1	0					
Totals	38	4	11	4		33	1	5	1

Philadelphia	0 0 0 0 0 1 0 0 0 3–4
Brooklyn	0 0 0 0 0 1 0 0 0 0–1

Philadelphia	IP	H	R	ER	BB	SO
Roberts (W)	10	5	1	1	3	2
Brooklyn	**IP**	**H**	**R**	**ER**	**BB**	**SO**
Newcombe (L)	10	11	4	4	2	3

E–none. DP–Philadelphia 1, Brooklyn 1. LOB–Philadelphia 7, Brooklyn 5. 2B–Reese. HR–Reese, Sisler. SF–Roberts. T–2:35. A–35,073.

Bobby Thomson

The Miracle of Coogan's Bluff

October 3, 1951 Polo Grounds

Home run hitters gain recognition in a variety of ways. Some are known for their work during an entire career or season. Others attract attention for their long-distance clouting in clusters. Still others are connected with one homer of special importance.

If there was ever a hitter whose name was indelibly linked to a single home run, it was Bobby Thomson. Given the circumstances, it is no wonder.

The date was October 3, 1951. The site was New York's storied Polo Grounds. Bottom of the ninth in the final game of a special postseason playoff to decide the National League pennant.

With two New York teams—bitter rivals for decades—involved, the game commanded the attention of an entire city. Beyond the city limits, though, and with the aid of one of national TV's early efforts, a whole country was watching.

The events leading up to the game were extraordinary. Brooklyn, in the midst of an 11-year run during which it would win six National League flags and lose three others on the final day of the season, had seemingly wrapped up the 1951 pennant early.

On the morning of August 11, the Dodgers had a 13½ game lead. The lead seemed so insurmountable that Brooklyn manager Charlie Dressen told his team, "We've knocked 'em [the second-place Giants] out of the race. They won't bother us anymore."

While the Dodgers played mediocre ball the rest of the way, winning 26 and losing 22 games, the Giants got hot. At one point winning 16 straight games, manager Leo Durocher's New York club won 37 of its last 44 regular-season games, steadily shaving the Dodgers lead until it pulled to a tie with two games of the season remaining for each team.

Brooklyn won its final two games, the last one coming on a heroic 14th-inning home run by Jackie Robinson. New York also won twice, sending the deadlocked teams into a special best-of-three playoff to decide the pennant.

In the first game, played at Ebbets Field, Thomson's two-run homer off Brooklyn starter Ralph Branca snapped a 1–1 tie and sent the Giants and Jim Hearn home with a 3–1 victory. Thomson, normally an outfielder who had been moved to third base early in the season, was conspicuous again in the second game at the Polo Grounds, making two errors and a base-running mistake as the Dodgers bounced back with a 10–0 victory behind Clem Labine.

The whole season boiled down to one final game at Polo Grounds, a winner-take-all proposition to determine who would face the New York Yankees in the World Series. A frenzied but surprisingly small crowd of 34,320 flocked to the Polo Grounds, affectionately called Coogan's Bluff by Giants fans, to watch the two teams that hated each other with a passion go at it.

With the Giants' Sal Maglie, a 23-game winner, facing Dodgers' 20-game winner Don Newcombe, Brooklyn drew first blood with one run in the first inning. The score remained 1–0 until the Giants tied it with a run in the seventh on a sacrifice fly to deep center by Thomson.

By then, Thomson, a native of Scotland who had grown up on New York's Staten Island, already had two hits, a second-inning single and a fifth-inning double. In the second, however, running with his head down, he had been thrown out, killing what could have been a Giants scoring opportunity.

The Dodgers appeared to break the game open in the top of the eighth, scoring three runs and routing Maglie to take a 4–1 lead. Soon afterward, a large gathering of writers assembled outside the Dodger locker room to report the postgame celebration.

But the contest wasn't over yet. After striking out the side in the eighth and yielding only four hits in the game, Newcombe issued a leadoff single to Al Dark in the ninth. Don Mueller followed with another single. Then, after Monte Irvin fouled out, Whitey Lockman sliced a double to left. Dark scored easily, but on the play, Mueller slid hard into third trying to beat Andy Pafko's throw and wound up with a broken ankle.

The wheels were turning as Mueller was carried off the field on a stretcher. Clint Hartung came in to run for the injured Giant. And Dressen, feeling Newcombe had had enough, summoned Branca from the bullpen to face Thomson.

"When Mueller got hurt, I ran down to third where he was lying," Thomson recalled. "I still had the bat in my hand. He was my friend. When I saw him lying there in pain, it got my mind totally off the game. I was more concerned for him. In fact, I didn't even know the Dodgers had made a pitching change until I got back to the plate."

Normally a starter, the hard-throwing Branca, had been warming up in the bullpen along with Carl Erskine and Labine. But bullpen coach Clyde Sukeforth recommed Branca over the others. "They told me he had a lot of stuff. That's why I called him," Dressen said later.

Thomson dug in against Branca. The soon-to-be-28-year-old right-handed slugger had become one of the National League's better hitters since breaking into the majors late in 1946. He had hit 97 home runs in his first four full seasons, and in 1951 he would swat 32 out of the park while carrying a .293 average.

"I'd never been in a spot like that, so I was talking to myself, telling myself to wait and watch," Thomson said. "I wasn't nervous. In a situation like that, you just follow your instincts. I was determined to hit the ball. I just wanted to do a good job in that situation, and I was concentrating totally."

Branca's first pitch was a fastball for a called strike. The next pitch was also a fastball, and Thomson got around on it and took a lusty swing. A searing line drive flew off the bat. Passing well above the reach of Dodger left fielder Pafko as he leaned against the wall, the ball sailed into the stands at the 315-foot sign for a three-run homer and a most improbable 5–4 Giants victory.

"At first, I thought the ball was going over the wall," said Thomson. "Then it started to sink. I thought, Oh Geez, it's not going to make it. Then when it did, I just started jumping up and down.

"Then I started running around the bases. Things were happening so fast, it was hard to realize what was going on. I was hyperventilating. Everything was just a blur."

Hartung and Lockman scored ahead of Thomson, who was followed around the bases by Robinson, making sure the Giants slugger touched each sack. With Durocher, a former Dodgers manager who had been coaching at third base, jumping wildly behind him, Thomson was engulfed by jubilant teammates as he reached home plate.

While Giants broadcaster Russ Hodges screamed over and over into the mike, "The Giants win the pennant, the Giants win the pennant," Thomson was half carried, half washed along in the tide of happy players to the team's clubhouse in center field. And all over Coogan's Bluff, bedlam reigned.

It was a different story in the tomb-like Dodger clubhouse. Teary-eyed players sat in shell-shocked silence. "We saw ourselves going to the World Series," Robinson summarized. "And then boom—five minutes later here we are just sitting in the clubhouse."

A grieving Branca, an excellent pitcher who had won 21 games as a 21-year-old in 1947, slumped over as he sat on a small set of steps, his head in his hands and tears streaming down his face. "It wasn't a bad pitch," he said finally. "I didn't think he hit it too well."

Later, Branca would pull himself together and talk more about the event. "I'll tell you one thing," he said. "They didn't send in the worst pitcher they had. They sent in their best pitcher in that spot."

Writers dubbed the game "The Miracle of Coogan's Bluff." Ultimately, the homer was called "The Shot Heard 'Round the World."

The blow gave the Giants their 16th pennant, but the first one since 1937.

In the World Series, the Giants lost in six games to the Yankees, a powerful club on the way to five straight world championships between 1949 and 1953.

For Thomson, it would be far and away the high point of a fine career. Bobby went on to play 15 seasons in the big leagues. But there was never anything close to equaling his mighty homer against the Dodgers.

Ironically, Thomson and Branca later became close friends. On occasion, they socialized together and sometimes even performed a skit together at banquets. "Ralph and I agree that we both would have been forgotten

Bobby Thomson celebrated his "Shot Heard 'Round the World" with Giants manager Leo Durocher (*left*).

long ago if it hadn't been for that home run," Thomson said. "I had one day in the sun, so to speak. You just have to be thankful for small blessings."

It was anything but small at the time. In fact, to this day, it remains the single most noteworthy home run ever hit.

Brooklyn	**AB**	**R**	**H**	**RBI**	**New York**	**AB**	**R**	**H**	**RBI**
Furillo, rf	5	0	0	0	Stanky, 2b	4	0	0	0
Reese, ss	4	2	1	0	Dark, ss	4	1	1	0
Snider, cf	3	1	2	0	Mueller, rf	4	0	1	0
Robinson, 2b	2	1	1	1	Hartung, pr	0	1	0	0
Pafko, lf	4	0	1	1	Irvin, lf	4	1	1	0
Hodges, 1b	4	0	0	0	Lockman, 1B	3	1	2	1
Cox, 3b	4	0	2	1	Thomson, 3b	4	1	3	4
Walker, c	4	0	1	0	Mays, cf	3	0	0	0
Newcombe, p	4	0	0	0	Westrum, c	0	0	0	0
Branca, p	0	0	0	0	Rigney, ph	1	0	0	0
					Noble, c	0	0	0	0
					Maglie, p	2	0	0	0
					Thompson, ph	1	0	0	0
					Jansen, p	0	0	0	0
Totals	34	4	8	3		30	5	8	5

Brooklyn 1 0 0 0 0 0 0 3 0 **4**
New York 0 0 0 0 0 0 1 0 4 **5**

One out when winning run scored

Brooklyn	**IP**	**H**	**R**	**ER**	**BB**	**SO**
Newcombe	8⅓	7	4	4	2	2
Branca (L)	0*	1	1	1	0	0
New York	**IP**	**H**	**R**	**ER**	**BB**	**SO**
Maglie	8	8	4	4	4	6
Jansen (W)	1	0	0	0	0	0

*Pitched to one batter in ninth.

E–None. DP–Brooklyn 2. LOB–Brooklyn 7, New York 3. 2B–Thomson, Irvin, Lockman. HR–Thomson. SH–Lockman. WP–Maglie. T–2:28. A–34,320.

Mickey Mantle

First of the Tape-Measure Homers

April 17, 1953 Griffith Stadium

No one aspect of baseball carries with it as much variety as a home run. Home runs come in all different shapes and sizes, and no two are ever entirely alike.

Some are searing line drives. Some are high, towering flies. Some never leave the park. Others barely slip over the fence. A few are crushed with such strength that they either leave the ballpark or land in one of its most distant regions.

Only a handful of players throughout baseball history have regularly hit home runs that have been noted for the distance they have traveled. One of them was Mickey Mantle.

Mantle belongs to a select group that includes such long-distance clouters as Babe Ruth, Jimmie Foxx, Josh Gibson, Dick Allen, Mark McGwire, and perhaps a few others. Of all the players associated with mammoth home runs, though, Mantle stands higher than the rest.

It was Mickey's massive blasts that have left the biggest mark. Mantle's long drives have become legendary. And those who saw them still discuss them with awe and point to the spots where they landed.

It has been said that Mantle's legacy to baseball was his prodigious home run clouts. Certainly, Mickey was the first player to prompt the use of a tape measure to calculate the distance a home run traveled. And just as surely, it was the Mick who seemed to hit more gigantic homers than anyone had ever done before.

Mantle's homers were regularly measured and reported. As noteworthy as the distance he hit them was the fact that the muscular center fielder could hit tape-measure shots from either side of the plate. No switch-hitter in baseball had ever hit with such power.

"I've never seen anything like it," the fabled manager Casey Stengel once said. "He can unload them like cannon shots from either side of the plate. Nobody ever did that before."

Nor has anybody done it since. Mantle ranks eighth on the all-time home run list with 536, and only one other switch-hitter—Eddie Murray with 504—comes close to Mickey's career total. Mantle is more than 200 homers above the total of the third-highest switch-hitter, Reggie Smith.

During a career that went from 1951 to 1968, the New York Yankees slugger won four home run crowns. Twice he hit more than 50 homers in a season, slashing 52 in 1956 and 54 in 1961 when he and Roger Maris waged their storied home run battle . Ten times he hit more than 30 home runs in a season.

Of all his many four-baggers, though, it was the big ones that drew the most attention. Mantle, who had a career batting average of .298, almost became the only batter ever to hit the ball out of Yankee Stadium, twice hitting the facade right below the roof, once in 1956 on a pitch by the Washington Senators' Pedro Ramos and another time in 1963 on a toss from the Kansas City A's Bill Fischer.

Mantle hit the longest ball ever measured at Yankee Stadium, a 502-foot blast. He cleared the right-field roof several times at Tiger Stadium in Detroit. He hit a mammoth 470-foot shot at Cleveland's Municipal Stadium. He smashed one at the base of the light tower atop the roof at Chicago's old Comiskey Park. And he slugged a 480-foot missile over two fences at Minnesota's Municipal Stadium.

These tape-measure clouts by the future Hall of Famer were just a few of the many that Mantle drilled during his 18 years of relentlessly pounding enemy pitching. Of all the ones he hit, though, none was more gigantic or attracted more attention than the one he crushed April 17, 1953, at Griffith Stadium in Washington.

It came back in the days when there were still only eight teams in each league, and the overall pitching was of considerably higher quality than it is in today's game where the mounds are infested with hurlers of no better than Double-A caliber. And it left hardened observers gasping in amazement, while wondering what spectacular slugging feat the young Oklahoma powerhouse would perform next.

The 1953 season had started just three days earlier, and although the weather was still chilly, Mantle was already starting to heat up. Just eight days earlier, he had belted a tremendous shot over the right field roof in an exhibition game at Forbes Field in Pittsburgh. Only two others players—one being Ruth—had ever done that before.

Before the game in Washington, Mickey put on a dazzling exhibition of long ball during batting practice. A strong wind was blowing toward left field as Chuck Stobbs took the mound in his first appearance for the Washington Senators. Stobbs was a lefthander who had lost one game the previous year while with the Chicago White Sox when he gave up a ninth-inning grand slam to Mantle. He was, however, a respectable moundsman who would win in double figures six times while hurling for mostly mediocre to weak teams during a 15-year big league career.

Billy Martin's home run gave the Yankees and Eddie Lopat a 1–0 lead in the third inning. The Senators came back to tie on Eddie Yost's RBI single in the bottom of the third. Then in the fourth, Hank Bauer doubled and scored on a single by Joe Collins to put the Yanks back in front, 2–1.

The fifth inning got under way with Stobbs setting down Martin and Phil Rizzuto. He then walked Yogi Berra. The next batter was Mantle.

Mickey had lined out to third and walked in his two previous trips to the plate. Now, batting righthanded, he took a mighty swing at Stobbs's second pitch—a letter-high fastball—and hit the ball squarely on the nose. Like a golf pro's two-iron shot, the ball flew off Mantle's bat, rising as it bore a searing path to left-center field.

The ball easily cleared the fence 391 feet from home and flew well over the 55-foot-high bleachers. It finally glanced off a beer sign on a Redskins football scoreboard that sat above the highest level of the bleachers and continued outside the park and out of sight.

When the ball left the park, it had already traveled 460 feet. But it was still in flight. It flew across Fifth Street, which paralleled the left-field wall, before eventually coming down in the backyard of a home on Oakdale Street.

A monstrous clout by **Mickey Mantle** was measured as having traveled 565 feet.

A crowd of only 4,206 was on hand to see the titanic blast. But fans and players alike watched in amazement as the home run traveled its lengthy course. It was the only ball ever hit over the left-field bleachers at Griffith Stadium.

"I've never seen a ball hit farther," Stengel said later. "I've seen a lot of home runs, but I've never seen anything like it."

As soon as it became apparent that the home run was something special, Yankees publicity director Arthur (Reds) Patterson raced from the press box in search of the spot where the ball landed. Eventually, he found a young boy holding what turned out to be the ball that Mantle had hit.

Patterson quizzed the youth about where the ball had landed. Then, after being shown the spot, the New York PR man paced off the distance between it and the outer wall. He concluded that the ball had traveled 565 feet. That would make it the longest home run ever measured.

"It was a tremendous hit," remembered Mickey Vernon, who was playing first base for the Senators when the ball was hit. "I just stood there and followed the flight of the ball. I think it would have gone even farther than it did if it hadn't touched the scoreboard.

"The longest home run ever hit before that at Griffith Stadium was one by Foxx," Vernon added. "I saw that, too. It landed three rows from the top of the bleachers. In fact, whenever anybody hit a long home run and people would be talking about how far it went, some of the old coaches would say, 'You think that's long. There's where Jimmie Foxx hit one.' It was quite a blow. But Mantle's went farther than that."

Mantle was unimpressed with his powerful blast. He said at first he didn't think he hit the ball well enough for it to go out. When Patterson gave him the ball he had retrieved, Mickey said he would send it home and his brothers would probably play with it.

Asked for his opinion, Stobbs said, "He really hit the hell out of it, didn't he?"

In his final two times at bat in the game, Mantle, now batting lefthanded, walked and poked a bunt for a hit. The Yanks walked off with a 7–3 victory.

The next day, the home run was being hailed as the longest ever hit. But a controversy quickly arose over the exact distance the ball traveled. Some found fault not only with Patterson's claim of 565 feet, but also with his sole reliance on a 10-year-old boy for his information.

In later years, others joined the fray, claiming that Patterson's distance was a gross exaggeration. Some pointed out, however, that the ball might have gone farther than the 565 feet had it not hit the beer sign on the scoreboard.

Regardless, there was no disputing the fact that it was a mammoth home run, surely one of the longest, if not the longest, ever hit. Hit by the master of long-distance belts, it ushered in the era of the tape-measure home run that continues to this day.

And it was without question one of the most stunningly spectacular home runs that ever left a ballpark.

New York	AB	R	H	RBI	Washington	AB	R	H	RBI
Martin, 2b	4	1	2	2	Yost, 3b	5	0	2	1
Rizzuto, ss	5	0	1	0	Busby, cf	4	0	1	0
Berra, c	4	1	1	0	Vernon, 1b	3	0	0	0
Mantle, cf	3	1	2	2	Jensen, rf	4	0	0	0
Bauer, rf	4	2	1	0	Runnels, ss	3	1	1	0
Woodling, lf	5	1	2	1	Wood, lf	4	0	1	0
Collins, 1b	4	0	1	1	Terwilliger, 2b	4	2	3	1
Carey, 3b	4	1	1	1	Peden, c	4	0	1	0
Lopat, p	4	0	1	0	Stobbs, p	1	0	0	0
Gorman, p	0	0	0	0	Moreno, p	0	0	0	0
					Hoderlein, ph	1	0	1	1
					Verble, ph	1	0	0	0
Totals	37	7	12	7		34	3	10	3

New York	0 0 1 1 2 0 0 3 0 **7**
Washington	0 0 1 0 0 0 1 1 0 **3**

New York	IP	H	R	ER	BB	SO
Lopat (W)	8	10	3	3	3	2
Gorman	1	0	0	0	0	0
Washington	**IP**	**H**	**R**	**ER**	**BB**	**SO**
Stobbs (L)	7	7	4	4	4	0
Moreno	2	5	3	3	2	0

E–None. 2B–Bauer, Terwilliger, Woodling. HR–Martin, Mantle. SB–Mantle. SF–Stobbs. DP–New York 1. LOB–New York 9, Washington 8. T–2:27. A–4,206.

Dusty Rhodes

Vaunted Indians Staff Goes Down

September 29, 1954 Polo Grounds

Unless it travels a prodigious distance, making it worthy of special attention, it doesn't matter how far a home run is hit. As long as it goes over the wall, one home run counts the same as the next.

A dinky homer that just makes it over the fence has the same impact as a mighty clout over the grandstand roof. Each allows the batter to circle the bases. Each counts as one run, no matter the length of the blast.

The home run that Robert (Dusty) Rhodes hit in the first game of the 1954 World Series traveled a meager 260 feet. Yet, because of the circumstances, it qualifies as one of baseball's most memorable four-baggers.

Rhodes's clout, which was followed by another key blow the next day, not only gave the unheralded batter a place in the hitting heroes' Valhalla, but it also launched his New York Giants toward one of the most stunning upsets in World Series history.

Unlike most other owners of memorable home runs, Rhodes was hardly a household name. More noted for his fun-loving habits and his willingness to imbibe, Dusty was a good-hit, horrendous-fielding outfielder whose best work was usually performed in the role of a pinch-hitter.

Dusty's glove was so bad that playing as a regular was out of the ques-

Heavy hitting by **Dusty Rhodes** led the Giants to a remarkable Series sweep.

tion, even though he did carry a big stick. In fact, Giants manager Leo Durocher once said of Rhodes, "He is the worst fielder who ever played in a big league game."

So Rhodes was confined mostly to the bench where he would wait to be summoned to the plate when a crucial situation was at hand. It was a role he relished, but not one that made him particularly prominent.

At least, not until the 1954 World Series. Then, Dusty had his moment in the sun.

The Series, pitting the Giants against the Cleveland Indians, was not expected to be much of a contest. The Indians were heavily favored, and experts predicted it would be a short Series.

There was good reason to favor Cleveland. En route to winning the American League pennant and ending the New York Yankees' streak of five straight flags, the Indians had set a new league record with 111 victories. It was the most victories for a major league team since 1906. Losing only 43 games, manager Al Lopez's Tribe was a marvelous combination of offense and defense.

Cleveland had one of the finest pitching staffs ever assembled. It featured 23-game winners Bob Lemon and Early Wynn, 19-game winner Mike Garcia, and a host of other strong arms including Art Houtteman, aging stars Bob Feller and Hal Newhouser, and a magnificent bullpen duo of Ray

Narleski and Don Mossi. Four of those hurlers (Lemon, Wynn, Feller, and Newhouser) now have a spot in the Hall of Fame.

The Indians also took the field with the 1954 American League batting champion, Bobby Avila; the AL home run and RBI king, Larry Doby; and a group of other big hitters including Al Rosen, Vic Wertz, and Al Smith, plus standout catcher Jim Hegan.

Although highly respectable, the Giants were hardly in the same category. After struggling in the early part of the season and not reaching .500 until May 22, they had won 97 games and captured the National League pennant by five games over the Brooklyn Dodgers. The incomparable Willie Mays, just back from a nearly two-year stint in the army, had won the National League batting championship, edging teammate Don Mueller and Brooklyn's Duke Snider on the final day of the season. The Giants also had dependable hitters in Al Dark, Monte Irvin, Hank Thompson, and Whitey Lockman. Johnny Antonelli, owner of 21 victories, headed a pitching staff that had no other big winner.

But the Giants weren't in the same class as the Indians, and many experts predicted a Series sweep as the event began to unfold on September 28 at New York's Polo Grounds. Lemon got the call for the Indians against 14-game winner Sal Maglie, a wily veteran on the downside of a short but fine career.

Wertz got the Indians off to a roaring start with a two-out, two-run triple in the first inning. The Giants came back to tie in the third with Thompson's RBI single being the key blow.

Cleveland threatened several times thereafter but was unable to score, and the 2–2 deadlock remained as the eighth inning began. Maglie was tiring, and his fatigue showed as he served up a leadoff walk to Doby followed by a single by Rosen. The lefthanded-batting Wertz, already 3-for-3 on the day, then came to the plate as Durocher called in southpaw Don Liddle to replace Maglie.

The red-hot Wertz quickly pounced on a Liddle pitch and slammed a screaming drive to deep center field. It looked like a certain extra-base hit, but Mays, racing straight back, made a sensational over-the-shoulder catch in front of the center-field wall, some 460 feet from the plate. Mays then wheeled, and threw back to the infield as Doby tagged up and moved to third. The breath-taking grab, which few would have believed possible, was immediately heralded as one of the greatest catches ever made.

With Marv Grissom now replacing the shaken Liddle, New York escaped the jam, but only after pinch-hitter Dale Mitchell had walked to load the bases. Finally, Grissom struck out Dave Pope, and Hegan hit a towering fly to deep left that was caught by Irvin.

The tie was preserved, and the score stayed that way, even though the Indians put two men on base in the ninth and Wertz smashed a double in the 10th for his fourth hit of the game.

As if they hadn't already had enough breaks, the Giants' luck continued in the bottom of the 10th. With one out, Mays walked, then stole second. Lopez ordered an intentional walk to Thompson with Irvin due to bat next.

But Durocher had another idea. He still had Rhodes on the bench. It was the ideal time to send Dusty to the plate.

In his third campaign, Rhodes had hit a glittering .341 during the season with 15 home runs and 50 RBI in just 164 at-bats. Dusty was also 15-for-45 as a pinch-hitter and had won more than one dozen games coming off the bench. "When the pressure was on, I couldn't wait to grab a bat and get to the plate," Rhodes said.

Now, he had a chance to do it again. Rhodes went up to the plate to bat for Irvin, and on the first pitch, a slow curve over the middle of the plate, he lofted a high fly down the right-field line. Few among the 52,751 in the stands thought it was anything but a big out.

But the Polo Grounds had a notorious right-field line that was a mere 257 feet from home plate. That was a joke by big league standards, but it was like found money for a pull-hitter like Rhodes.

As Pope attempted a futile leap to make the catch, the ball just escaped his outstretched glove and flew over the 11-foot-high wall, landing in the first row of the right-field bleachers. The ball had traveled no more than 260 feet, but it was a home run, nonetheless, and it gave the Giants a stunning 5–2 victory.

The Indians were aghast. Lemon flung his glove in the air and stomped off the mound. "In our park, the right fielder would have moved in to catch that ball," he fumed. "I thought it was just another out, but all at once the game's over. It sure is tough to lose a game on a hit like that."

Lopez could hardly believe what he saw. "I thought it was just a routine out when it left the bat," he said. "But the wind caught it a little. It went for a home run, and there's no defense against home runs."

Of all the memorable home runs that have embellished the game of baseball, this one was the shortest. Cheap though it might have been, it still provided baseball with one of its most dramatic moments. "A home run is a home run," Rhodes said in defense of his blast. "That's all that matters."

Dusty wasn't quite through. The following day, he stroked a fifth inning pinch-hit single to drive in a run. Then, left in the game, he blasted a solo homer against the facade in right field in the seventh to lead the Giants and Antonelli to a 3–1 victory.

In the third game at Cleveland's Municipal Stadium, Rhodes whacked a two-run, pinch-hit single in the third inning to put the Giants ahead in an eventual 6–2 triumph. He didn't play in the fourth game, but the Giants won again, 7–4, to complete an astonishing sweep that is generally considered one of the biggest upsets in a World Series.

With four hits in six at-bats, including two home runs, and with seven RBI, Rhodes had played a major part in the victory, the last bright moment in New York for the Giants, who would move to San Francisco after the 1957 season.

Dusty continued his lusty hitting in 1955, compiling a .305 batting average. But he faded quickly after that, eventually winding up back in the minors in 1958. After a brief stint back with the Giants in 1959, he was released. It was the end of Rhodes' short career in the big leagues.

But because of a hit that traveled no farther than an ordinary pop fly, that barely made it over the wall, and that started his team on the way to a stunning upset victory in a World Series, Rhodes' name is forever linked with baseball's most memorable home runs.

Cleveland	AB	R	H	RBI	New York	AB	R	H	RBI
Smith, lf	4	1	1	0	Lockman, 1b	5	1	1	0
Avila, 2b	5	1	1	0	Dark, ss	4	0	2	0
Doby, cf	3	0	1	0	Mueller, rf	5	1	2	1
Rosen, 3b	5	0	1	0	Mays, cf	3	1	0	0
Wertz, 1b	5	0	4	2	Thompson, 3b	3	1	1	1
Regalado, pr	0	0	0	0	Irvin, lf	3	0	0	0
Grasso, c	0	0	0	0	Rhodes, ph	1	1	1	3
Philley, rf	3	0	0	0	Williams, 2b	4	0	0	0
Majeski, ph	0	0	0	0	Westrum, c	4	0	2	0
Mitchell, ph	0	0	0	0	Maglie, p	3	0	0	0
Dente, ss	0	0	0	0	Liddle, p	0	0	0	0
Strickland, ss	3	0	0	0	Grissom, p	1	0	0	0
Pope, ph, rf	1	0	0	0					
Hegan, c	4	0	0	0					
Glynn, ph, 1b	1	0	0	0					
Lemon, p	4	0	0	0					
Totals	38	2	8	2		36	5	9	5

Cleveland	2 0 0 0 0 0 0 0 0 0 **2**
New York	0 0 2 0 0 0 0 0 0 3 **5**

One out when winning run scored

Cleveland	IP	H	R	ER	BB	SO
Lemon (L)	9⅓	9	5	5	5	6
New York	**IP**	**H**	**R**	**ER**	**BB**	**SO**
Maglie	7*	7	2	2	2	2
Liddle	⅓	0	0	0	0	0
Grissom (W)	2⅔	1	0	0	3	2

*Pitched to two batters in eighth

E–Mueller 2, Irvin. LOB–Cleveland 13, New York 9. 2B–Wertz. 3B–Wertz. HR–Rhodes. SB-Mays. SH–Irvin, Dente. HBP–By Maglie (Smith). WP–Lemon. T–3:11. A–52,751.

Ted Williams

Bowing Out in Grand Style

September 28, 1960 Fenway Park

There can be no grander way for a hitter to conclude a storied career than by slugging a home run in his final trip to the plate. It is the perfect way to slip off into the sunset.

The crowd is on its feet cheering. The atmosphere drips heavily with sentiment. A few tears have spilled. And then in one last emotional burst of drama, a ball flies off the bat and soars into the distant bleachers. What a way to go out.

That is precisely the way that Ted Williams went out at the conclusion of a magnificent 19-year career. In the eighth inning of a September 28, 1960, game at Fenway Park, the 42-year-old Boston Red Sox slugger inscribed one final exclamation mark on his record with a solo homer against the Baltimore Orioles.

For Williams, it was not only his 521st home run, which at the time placed him third on the all-time list behind Babe Ruth and Jimmie Foxx, but it was also one of the two biggest thrills of his career. "That and the home run that won the 1941 All-Star Game at Briggs Stadium in Detroit were the two moments I remember most fondly," Williams said. "That last home run did a little something different to me. I felt it a little bit more."

Special moments were, of course, virtually a trademark of Williams' Hall of Fame career. The Red Sox legend began performing noteworthy feats nearly as soon as he arrived in the big leagues in 1939, a fresh, skinny kid who had once been a pitcher.

En route to tying for the sixth-highest batting average (.344) in big league history and ranking second on the all-time list in slugging percentage with a .634, the man who became baseball's last .400 hitter when he hit .406 in 1941 led the American League in hitting six times while hitting .300 or above 16 times. At the age of 39 in 1957, he led the league with a remarkable .388 average. One year later, he won again with a .328 mark.

The home run was a particularly prominent part of Williams' arsenal. Generally considered the finest hitter ever to play the game, the two-time Triple Crown winner led the league in homers four times and blasted 30 or more homers in a season eight times. Along the way, he hit many memorable four-baggers.

The Splendid Splinter, as the lefthanded batsman was nicknamed, not only hit a dramatic three-run, ninth-inning home run to win the 1941 All-Star Game, but he smacked another memorable blast off Rip Sewell's famed blooper pitch in the 1946 All-Star Game. Williams also hit a memorable inside-the-park homer in 1946 to beat the Boudreau Shift, 1–0, and he drilled a game-winning homer against the Detroit Tigers in his final trip to the plate before reporting in 1952 for active duty as a U.S. Marine pilot in the Korean War, one of two military stints that cost him nearly five years of his playing career.

But there was no home run more dramatic than the one he hit to close out his career in 1960.

After he'd hit a meager .254 in 1959, the Red Sox had tried to talk Williams into retiring, but Ted adamantly refused. Instead, he returned for another season, the Red Sox hoping to use him mostly as a pinch-hitter.

Despite some physical problems, including a pulled leg muscle, a neck problem, and a nagging virus that were joined by the usual aches and pains of the aging process, Williams managed to play in 113 games. And he showed without a doubt that he could still hit.

In his first time at bat on opening day, he smashed a 500-foot homer off the Washington Senators' Camilo Pascual. It was one of the longest homers Williams ever hit. The next day, he homered again. Then on June 17 he became only the fourth player at the time to hit 500 career home runs when he reached the lofty milestone against the Cleveland Indians' Wayne Hawkins.

For a man who that summer would become 42 years old, Williams was having an amazing season. But the best was yet to come. It occurred on a cold, dark, dreary day when rain posed a constant threat.

Williams had not told anyone except Boston general manager Mike Higgins that this would be his last game. In fact, the Red Sox still had a three-game series in New York before concluding the season. But it was no secret that Ted was about to retire.

"I had had it," he said. "I had gone as far as I could. When I arrived at the park that day, I said to Higgins, 'Mike, this is the last game I'm going to play. I don't want to go to New York.' "

A small ceremony was held at home plate before the game. Broadcaster Curt Gowdy, announcing the proceedings, called Williams "the greatest hitter who ever lived" and "a champion of sports." Boston mayor John Collins declared it "Ted Williams Day." After receiving a silver bowl, a plaque, and a donation to his pet project—the Jimmy Fund—Williams watched as the Red Sox announced that they were retiring his number 9.

Ted responded with a short statement, which thanked the Red Sox, their owner Tom Yawkey, and the fans, and in typical Williams fashion took a shot at the press. He then walked to the dugout as the fans stood and applauded.

Williams had taken no batting practice before the game. He stood with the bat on his shoulder as the Orioles' Steve Barber walked him on four pitches in his first trip to the plate. In the third, reliever Jack Fisher got Ted on a high fly to Jackie Brandt in deep center.

Ted's third at-bat came in the fifth, and he drilled a screaming drive to deep right-center. Baltimore right fielder Al Pilarcik raced to the base of the wall and made a chest-high catch some 400 feet from home plate. The fans gave Williams a standing ovation as he returned to the dugout.

"If that one didn't go out, none of them will today," Williams said to teammate Vic Wertz in the dugout. "I really stung it."

Williams' next at-bat was in the eighth inning. It would be his last trip to the plate, and as soon as he approached the on-deck circle, the fans were on their feet cheering again.

With the park lights now turned on, and the Red Sox trailing, 4–2, Willie Tasby grounded out to start the inning. Then Ted stepped into the

No one ever retired in finer fashion than **Ted Williams** with his career-ending home run.

batter's box. A two-minute ovation followed, stopping only after the righthanded Fisher had thrown the first pitch for a ball.

Williams swung and missed at the next pitch. Then Fisher came back with a waist-high fastball on the outside corner. Ted snapped at it, and from the moment he hit it, everyone among the sparse crowd of 10,454 knew it was gone.

The ball, a high, towering drive, bored through the thick air, refusing to stop until it cleared the wall in right-center field, landing above the bullpen. Williams circled the bases quickly, accompanied by a deafening roar of the crowd that lasted nearly five minutes before play was resumed.

"I was gunning for the big one," he told reporters afterward. "I let everything I had go. I really wanted that one.

"I knew I had really given it a ride," Williams added. "It fought the wind, and it just kept going and going, and then it went out. The fans reacted like nothing I've ever heard. As I came around first, I thought about tipping my hat, but by the time I got to second base, I knew I couldn't do it. It just wouldn't have been me.

"But you can't imagine the warm feeling I had for the very fact that I had done what every ballplayer would want to do on his last trip up. I had wanted to do it so badly."

Williams took his place in left field to start the top of the ninth, but as soon as he got there, Carroll Hardy arrived to replace him. As they fans cheered wildly, Ted trotted off the field with his head down.

Living up to his cantankerous image, he said he had no feelings as he ran off the field. "I felt nothing," he said. "Nothing, nothing, nothing."

Boston rallied with two runs in the bottom of the ninth to win the game, 5–4. Williams retired to the comfort of the locker room. No special celebration took place, and eventually, after answering reporters' questions, Ted exited through a side entrance to avoid the crowd.

As planned, he would not make the season-ending trip to New York. His career was officially over.

Williams finished his final season with a .316 batting average and 29 home runs. For the great Boston slugger, a brilliant career had ended in the most dramatic fashion imaginable.

Baltimore	AB	R	H	RBI	Boston	AB	R	H	RBI
Brandt, cf	5	0	0	0	Green, ss	3	0	0	0
Pilarcik, rf	4	0	1	0	Tasby, cf	4	1	0	1
Robinson, 3b	4	1	1	0	Williams, lf	3	2	1	1
Gentile, 1b	3	1	1	1	Hardy, lf	0	0	0	0
Triandos, c	4	1	2	2	Pagliaroni, c	3	0	2	0
Hansen, ss	4	1	2	0	Malzone, 3b	3	0	0	0
Stephens, lf	4	0	2	0	Clinton, rf	3	0	0	1
Breeding, 2b	2	0	0	0	Gile, 1b	4	0	0	0
Woodling, ph	1	0	0	1	Coughtry, 2b	3	1	2	0
Pearson, pr	0	0	0	0	Muffett, p	2	0	0	0
Klaus, 2b	1	0	0	0	Nixon, ph	1	0	0	0
Barber, p	0	0	0	0	Fornieles, p	0	0	0	0
Fisher, p	4	0	0	0	Wertz, ph	1	0	1	0
					Brewer, pr	0	1	0	0
Totals	36	4	9	4		30	5	6	3

Baltimore	0	2	0	0	1	1	0	0	0	**4**
Boston	2	0	0	0	0	0	0	1	2	**5**

Two outs when winning run scored

Baltimore	IP	H	R	ER	BB	SO
Barber	⅓	0	2	2	3	0
Fisher (L)	8⅓	6	3	2	3	5
Boston	**IP**	**H**	**R**	**ER**	**BB**	**SO**
Muffett	7	9	4	4	0	4
Fornieles (W)	2	0	0	0	0	2

E–Coughtry, Klaus. DP–Baltimore 1. LOB–Baltimore 6, Boston 7. 2B–Stephens, Robinson, Wertz. HR–Triandos, Williams. HBP–By Barber (Pagliaroni). WP–Barber, Muffett. T–2:18. A–10,454.

Bill Mazeroski

Biggest Blast in World Series History

October 13, 1960 Forbes Field

It is no small touch of irony that one of the most dramatic home runs ever hit came off the bat of a slick-fielding second baseman who was known particularly for his defense.

Bill Mazeroski was a master fielder, an eight-time Gold Glove winner with sure hands, superb range, and a deadly accurate arm. The Pittsburgh Pirates keystone sacker still holds major league records at his position for most doubleplays in a career (1,706) and a season (161) and most years leading the league in assists (nine).

So adept at whisking balls to first on the front end of doubleplay with such catlike quickness that it seemed he barely handled the ball, Mazeroski was often called "No Touch." It was a fitting nickname for a man who was generally regarded as one of the best, if not *the* best, defensive second baseman there ever was.

The compact, 5–11, 190-pound native of Wheeling, West Virginia, was no slouch at the plate, either. Although he ranks well behind Joe Morgan, Rogers Hornsby, and Ryne Sandberg, his 138 career home runs comprise the fourth-highest total among National League second basemen.

In a big league career that went from 1956 to 1972—all with the

Pirates—Mazeroski had a career batting average of .260 with 2,016 regular-season hits. Maz, who was named to seven All-Star teams, rarely sat out a contest, averaging 150 games per season during a 12-year stretch at the height of his career.

The high point of that career came in a thunderous moment on October 13, 1960, when Mazeroski blasted a ninth-inning home run in the seventh game of the World Series to give the Pirates a 10–9 victory over the New York Yankees at Pittsburgh's Forbes Field. The win gave the Pirates their first world championship in 35 years.

The Yankees, a team packed with outstanding players, including future Hall of Famers Mickey Mantle, Yogi Berra, and Whitey Ford, had been heavily favored to win the Series after using a 15-game winning streak late in the season to capture the American League pennant by eight games. Manager Casey Stengel's Yanks were making their 11th appearance in the fall classic in the last 14 years.

The Pirates, in contrast, had last appeared in the Series in 1927 when they were demolished by the Yankees and their legendary Murderers' Row in four straight games. After finishing in fourth place in 1959, the Bucs had romped to the National League pennant in 1960, winning the flag by seven games.

"Nobody thought we could beat the Yankees because they had Mantle, [Roger] Maris, Berra, and all those other big sluggers," Mazeroski recalled years later. "But we had a pretty good team, too. We didn't have a lot of power. But we had good starting pitching and good relieving. And we did little things that worked well. Whatever it took to win, we did it."

By the time Mazeroski hit his dramatic homer, the '60 Series had already been one that was almost too bizarre to believe. New York had won games by scores of 16–3, 10–0 and 12–0, while in three low-scoring games, Pittsburgh had won games by three runs, two runs, and one run. The Yankees were not only outscoring the Pirates by a huge overall margin, but they were outhitting them in overwhleming fashion as well (ultimately, 91–60) en route to amassing the highest team batting average (.338) for seven games in Series history.

Mazeroski had a big hand in two of the Pirates' early victories. His two-run, fourth-inning homer provided the winning margin in the Bucs' 6–4 victory in the first game. And his two-run double gave Pittsburgh the go-ahead runs in a 5–2 triumph in the fifth game. While the wins had gone to

Vern Law and Harvey Haddix, both games had been saved by the ubiquitous Elroy Face, who also saved the Bucs' and Law's 3–2 victory in the fourth game.

Pittsburgh, under colorful manager Danny Murtaugh, was known throughout the season for its ability to bounce back when the chips were down. But hardly anyone expected the Bucs to recover from the demoralizing, 17-hit, 12–0 thumping the Yanks gave them in the sixth game of the Series when Ford pitched his second shutout.

As Game 7 got under way, though, the Pirates were up to their old tricks. With the workhorse Law squaring off against 1958 Cy Young Award winner Bob Turley, who got the decision in the second game, Pittsburgh jumped out to a 2–0 lead on the strength of Rocky Nelson's two-run homer. Scoring twice more in the second on Bill Virdon's two-run single, the Pirates appeared to be in the driver's seat as they took a 4–1 advantage into the sixth.

But Law was weakening, and when he was replaced by an overworked Face, the Yankees had their opening. By the time the inning was over, Berra's three-run homer off Face had vaulted the Yankees to a 5–4 lead. New York then added two more runs off Face in the seventh, and the Yanks began icing the champagne.

It wasn't over yet. Down 7–4, the persistent Pirates exploded with five runs in the bottom of the eighth to regain the lead at 9–7. The Bucs got a big break when, after a leadoff, pinch-hit single by Gino Cimoli, a sure doubleplay grounder by Virdon took a bad hop and bounced into the throat of Tony Kubek, knocking the Yankee shortstop down and out of the game and giving the Pirates two men on base. Dick Groat and Roberto Clemente followed with RBI singles. Then reserve catcher Hal Smith seemingly earned a spot in World Series immortality with a three-run homer off Jim Coates.

The Yankees were bloodied, but hardly bowed. With all the grit of the great team they were, they stormed back with two runs in the top of the ninth. The Pirates tried to squash the rally, sending first Bob Friend, then Harvey Haddix—both starters—to the mound. But an RBI single by Mantle was followed by another run as Gil McDougald raced home from third on Berra's torrid smash on which Nelson gloved the ball at first but failed to make a play on what could have been an inning-ending doubleplay.

With the score tied at 9–9, the stage was set for Mazeroski, the number

Bill Mazeroski's home run at Forbes Field concluded an amazing comeback by the Pirates.

eight hitter in the lineup who was leading off the bottom of the ninth. Ralph Terry, the fifth Yankee pitcher of the game, threw a fastball for a ball. Then he grooved one up in the strike zone. Mazeroski turned on it, hammering a drive over the left-center-field wall.

Mazeroski said he hit a high fastball. "Terry said it was a high slider," Maz claimed. "If it was, it didn't slide.

"I didn't think the ball was going to go out," he added. "I thought it would be off the wall. I was digging all the way. I didn't actually see the ball go out. But when I saw Yogi [playing left field] give up on it, I knew it was out."

Mazeroski danced ecstatically around the bases, batting helmet in his hand. By the time he approached third base, many delirious Pirate fans from the crowd of 36,683 were already pouring out of the stands. Some followed him as he raced the final 90 feet to home where his teammates waited gleefully to congratulate him.

"By the time he got to the plate, all hell was breaking loose," recalled Mickey Vernon, who was coaching at first base for the Pirates that day. "Everybody was going crazy."

Soon the whole city of Pittsburgh was celebrating. Pandemonium erupted. People poured into the streets, auto horns blared, and the drinks started to flow in what many said was the wildest party ever held in the Steel City.

"I was really happy," Mazeroski recalled. "I was just so glad we beat the Yankees. I had thought we were going to lose when they tied it up in the top of the ninth."

Inside the raucous Pirates clubhouse, a 14-year-old boy named Andy Jerpe approached Mazeroski. He had caught the home run ball and was offering to give it to the Pirates hero.

Mazeroski signed the ball, and handed it back to the boy. "You keep it, son," he said. "The memory is good enough for me."

In the aftermath of the game, Stengel was relieved one week later of his duties as Yankees manager. For the Yanks, the '60 Series would be the first of five straight trips to the autumn festival. Terry would become the hero of the 1962 World Series against the San Francisco Giants, winning two games, including a 1–0 decision on a four-hitter in the seventh game.

The Pirates would not appear in another World Series until they beat the Baltimore Orioles in seven games in 1971. Mazeroski, who someday should earn a well-deserved spot in the Hall of Fame, went on to a stellar 17-year career—and everlasting recognition as the man who hit the most memorable home run in World Series history.

New York	AB	R	H	RBI	Pittsburgh	AB	R	H	RBI
Richardson, 2b	5	2	2	0	Virdon, cf	4	1	2	2
Kubek, ss	3	1	0	0	Groat, ss	4	1	1	1
DeMaestri, ss	0	0	0	0	Skinner, lf	2	1	0	0
Long, ph	1	0	1	0	Nelson, 1b	3	1	1	2
McDougald, 3b	0	1	0	0	Clemente, rf	4	1	1	1
Maris, rf	5	0	0	0	Burgess, c	3	0	2	0
Mantle, cf	5	1	3	2	Christopher, pr	0	0	0	0
Berra, lf	4	2	1	4	Smith, c	1	1	1	3
Skowron, 1b	5	2	2	1	Hoak, 3B	3	1	0	0
Blanchard, c	4	0	1	1	Mazeroski, 2b	4	2	2	1
Boyer, 3b, ss	4	0	1	1	Law, p	2	0	0	0
Turley, p	0	0	0	0	Face, p	0	0	0	0
Stafford, p	0	0	0	0	Cimoli, ph	1	1	1	0
Lopez, ph	1	0	1	0	Friend, p	0	0	0	0
Shantz, p	3	0	1	0	Haddix, p	0	0	0	0
Coates, p	0	0	0	0					
Terry, p	0	0	0	0					
Totals	40	9	13	9		31	10	11	10

New York	0	0	0	0	1	4	0	2	2	**9**
Pittsburgh	2	2	0	0	0	0	0	5	1	**10**

New York	IP	H	R	ER	BB	SO
Turley	1*	2	3	3	1	0
Stafford	1	2	1	1	1	0
Shantz	5†	4	3	3	1	0
Coates	⅔	2	2	2	0	0
Terry (L)	⅓	1	1	1	0	0
Pittsburgh	**IP**	**H**	**R**	**ER**	**BB**	**SO**
Law	5‡	4	3	3	1	0
Face	3	6	4	4	1	0
Friend	0**	2	2	2	0	0
Haddix (W)	1	1	0	0	0	0

*Pitched to one batter in second.
†Pitched to two batters in sixth.
‡Pitched to three batters in eighth.
**Pitched to two batters in ninth.

E–Maris. DP–New York 3. LOB–New York 6, Pittsburgh 1. 2B–Boyer. HR–Nelson, Skowron, Berra, Smith, Mazeroski. SH–Skinner. T–2:36. A–36,683.

Roger Maris

A Special Record Is Broken

October 1, 1961 Yankee Stadium

Under ordinary circumstances, there is no more popular player than a home run hitter. He's the guy the fans cheer loudest, other players admire the most, and the press glamorizes more than anybody.

When Roger Maris hit 61 homers in 1961, however, it was hardly under ordinary circumstances. The 27-year-old lefthanded slugger performed in conditions that were anything but normal.

In fact, when Maris blasted his memorable, record-breaking 61st homer on October 1, 1961, it's likely that no hitter ever performed under more adverse conditions. The fact that he succeeded, though, makes Maris's feat all the more impressive.

As a person, the quiet New York Yankees right fielder was a likable enough guy. It was the record he was chasing that caused him problems. Babe Ruth's 60 home runs in 1927 were regarded as the most sacred record in baseball. Only a heretic would break the record, many people felt, and when Maris began making his move toward the mark, he encountered widespread opposition.

Maris was not the first one to offer a serious challenge to Ruth's record. Jimmie Foxx in 1932 and Hank Greenberg in 1938 had each hit 58 homers, and Hack Wilson had hit 56 in 1930. Baseball purists breathed sighs of relief when they fell short.

Unlike the earlier bashers, Maris, operating in an age of heightened scrutiny, was much more vulnerable to the impulses of those who watched him. And watch him they did, not only in New York but throughout the world.

Maris was not used to all the attention. He had grown up in the quiet town of Fargo, North Dakota, a four-sport star in high school. Forgoing a football scholarship to the University of Oklahoma, he had entered the ranks of pro baseball in 1953, finally arriving in the big leagues with the Cleveland Indians in 1957. The following year he was traded to the Kansas City Athletics, who dealt him as part of a seven-player deal at the end of 1959 to the Yankees.

In 1960, Maris hammered 39 home runs—11 more than his previous high—hit .283, and led the American League in RBI with 112. At the end of the year, he was voted the league's Most Valuable Player.

More of the same was expected of Maris in 1961, and he didn't disappoint. He hit 11 home runs in May, 15 more in June, and 13 in July. All the while, he was waging a torrid duel with teammate Mickey Mantle for the home run leadership. The fans and press rooted for Mantle. "They favored Mickey," Maris said some years later. "I was never the fair-haired boy."

The race intensified, and by the end of July, Maris led, 40–39. Thinking that Ruth's record was in jeopardy, commissioner Ford Frick, a friend and former ghost writer of the ex-Yankee slugger, ruled that because the Babe set his record in 154 games and the current season lasted 162 games, an asterisk would be placed alongside the name of whoever broke Ruth's mark.

Such an insult merely added to the controversy that now swirled around the home run race. It was a controversy that not only included a ficticious story of a feud between close friends Maris and Mantle, but such constant abuse and pressure were directed especially toward Roger that he began losing his hair and showing other signs of fatigue, irritation, and nervousness.

"It was wasn't so much the pressure that was the problem," Maris said years later. "The big problem was the media. They created the pressure. It didn't matter that it was New York. The pressure would have been the same anywhere."

Maris was bombarded with constant and often absurd questions by the hordes of media types who besieged him before and after every game. "Can you break the record?" he was frequently asked. "I don't care about the damn record," he would reply. "All I'm interested in is winning the pennant."

There were constant comparisons between Ruth and Maris with the latter always coming out on the underside. Those affronts, along with other inanities such as the realization that people did not want him to break a hallowed 34-year-old record, made Maris increasingly unpleasant.

"I don't want to be Babe Ruth," he said. "I'm not trying to replace him. Ruth was a great man. Maybe I'm not a great man. But I damn well want to break the record. I guess that's something I'm not supposed to do."

The Yanks of 1961 were one of the great teams in the club's history and would win 109 games before crushing the Cincinnati Reds in a five-game World Series. But most of the attention was diverted to the Maris-Mantle battle.

Maris led, 51–48, in late August. Then in early September, Mantle fell ill with a virus, was eventually hospitalized and faded from the race, leaving pursuit of Ruth's record all to Maris.

No player in baseball history had ever hit 50 home runs by the end of August. Nor had anyone's nerves been so rawly exposed. But Maris, often surly, seldom with any peace or privacy, often booed by the fans, and in Detroit even showered with garbage, forged onward.

His homers tapered off. It took him until September 20—the day the Yankees clinched the pennant—to hit his 59th home run off Milt Papas in the 155th game at Baltimore's Memorial Stadium. He needed four more games and six days before clubbing no. 60 off the Orioles' Jack Fisher into the upper deck in right field at Yankee Stadium.

Maris still had four games to play. But the record-breaking home run eluded him. It all came down to the final game of the season on October 1 at Yankee Stadium.

The opponent was the Boston Red Sox. On the mound for the Bosox was rookie righthander Tracy Stallard, owner of a 2–6 record. An unbelievably small crowd of 23,154 was on hand to watch Maris's final assault on the record.

Maris, batting third in the order, flew out to deep left in his first trip to the plate. Roger, who vowed he would come out of the dugout swinging, came up again in the fourth. Stallard's first two pitches were balls. The

With one big swing, **Roger Maris** broke the home run record of a legend.

third pitch was a waist-high fastball. Maris turned on it and connected solidly, lashing a drive that didn't stop until it had landed 15 rows into the right-field stands, about 360 feet from home.

A new record had been set, asterisk and all. After watching the ball disappear, Roger romped blankly around the bases. The crowd cheered for five minutes. The home run turned out to be the only run of the game as the Yankees took a 1–0 decision.

"If I never hit another home run, this is one they can never take away from me," Maris said. "It gives me a wonderful feeling to know that I'm the only man in history to hit 61 home runs. It was the biggest home run I ever hit, even bigger than my 60th. I knew it was gone the minute I hit it."

Although he would be forever remembered as the pitcher who served up the record-breaking homer, Stallard viewed the situation calmly. "I don't feel badly about it," he told reporters. "Why should I? The guy hit 60 home runs off a bunch of other pitchers in the league before he got me. I gave him my best fastball, and he hit it."

Maris, who struck out against Stallard and popped out against Chet Nichols in his final two plate appearances, finished the season with league-leading totals in RBI (142) and runs scored (132) while batting .269. After the season, he was again voted the league's Most Valuable Player.

As it turned out, the asterisk controversy was highly unnecessary. Maris made 590 official trips to the plate. When he hit his 60th homer in the 154th game of the season, Ruth had come to bat 540 times. Overall, Ruth went to the plate 692 times (with 138 walks and 14 sacrifices included) to Maris's 698 (95 walks, seven sacrifices, six hit-by-a-pitch). Ruth hit his 60th homer in his 689th appearance, while Maris hit No. 60 in his 684th trip to the plate.

Mantle finished with 54 home runs, giving him and Maris the highest total (115) of round-trippers of any twosome in baseball history. Adding Bill Skowron's 28 homers, the Yanks also had baseball's most prooductive threesome with 143 four-baggers.

Maris, an accomplished fielder and an excellent base-runner who was a far better all-around player than he ever got credit for being, added another home run in the World Series. But he never had another year like the one he had in 1961.

He played through the 1966 season with the Yankees, never hitting more than 33 home runs in a season. He spent the last two years of his 12-

year major league career with the St. Louis Cardinals before retiring in 1968 with 275 career home runs and a .260 lifetime batting average.

"The 1961 season was a fine year, and it made my career," he once said. No one could argue with that statement. It was a year that belonged to Roger Maris, no matter what anybody else said or thought.

Boston	**AB**	**R**	**H**	**RBI**	**New York**	**AB**	**R**	**H**	**RBI**
Schilling, 2b	4	0	1	0	Richardson, 2b	4	0	0	0
Geiger, cf	4	0	0	0	Kubek, ss	4	0	2	0
Yastrzemski, lf	4	0	1	0	Maris, cf	4	1	1	1
Malzone, 3b	4	0	0	0	Berra, lf	2	0	0	0
Clinton, rf	4	0	0	0	Lopez, rf, lf	1	0	0	0
Runnels, 1b	3	0	0	0	Blanchard, rf, c	3	0	0	0
Gile, 1b	0	0	0	0	Howard, c	2	0	0	0
Nixon, c	3	0	2	0	Reed, lf	1	0	1	0
Green, ss	2	0	0	0	Skowron, 1b	2	0	0	0
Stallard, p	1	0	0	0	Hale, 1b	1	0	1	0
Jensen, ph	1	0	0	0	Boyer, 3b	2	0	0	0
Nichols, p	0	0	0	0	Stafford, p	2	0	0	0
					Reniff, p	0	0	0	0
					Tresh, ph	1	0	0	0
					Arroyo, p	0	0	0	0
Totals	30	0	4	0		29	1	5	1

Boston	0 0 0 0 0 0 0 0 0 **0**
New York	0 0 0 1 0 0 0 0 x **1**

Boston	**IP**	**H**	**R**	**ER**	**BB**	**SO**
Stallard (L)	7	5	1	1	1	5
Nichols	1	0	0	0	0	0
New York	**IP**	**H**	**R**	**ER**	**BB**	**SO**
Stafford (W)	6	3	0	0	1	7
Reniff	1	0	0	0	0	1
Arroyo	2	1	0	0	0	1

E–None. LOB–Boston 5, New York 5. 2B–Nixon. HR–Maris. SB–Geiger. SF–Stallard. WP–Stallard. PB–Nixon. T–1:57. A–23,154.

Hank Aaron

Baseball Gets a New Home Run King

April 8, 1974 Atlanta–Fulton County Stadium

It is a common practice in sports to build up a particularly important event before it happens. Stir the pot of excitement, elevate the level of anticipation, make it seem as though all attention is absolutely obligated to focus on what must surely be the most important occurrence ever to take place on the planet.

Most of the time, it's all just hype. Useless flotsam and jetsam. Public relations drivel.

A shining example to the contrary, however, took place as Hank Aaron approached his record-breaking 715th career home run. Few events in sports were ever as widely discussed or as eagerly anticipated. And equally few events ever turned out so fulfilling.

The record of 714 career home runs was held by Babe Ruth. Achieved nearly 40 years earlier in 1935, the record not only was considered one of baseball's most hallowed marks, but was also regarded as one of the records of the game least likely to be broken.

Of all of baseball's great home runs hitters since Ruth, none had come close to approaching the standard until Aaron came along. But by 1973 it had become apparent that the righthanded slugger from Mobile, Alabama, would likely smash the mark.

Since emerging as a skinny teenager from the dying days of the Negro

League to join the Milwaukee Braves in 1954, Aaron had averaged more than 35 home runs a season for 20 years. He had hit as many as 47 in one season, eight times had hit 40 or more, and four times had led the National League in home runs. His home run in 1957 had clinched the first pennant in Milwaukee.

In 1970, by then as a member of the Atlanta Braves, who left Milwaukee after the 1965 season, Aaron had also collected his 3,000th career hit. Having already hit more than 500 home runs, he was the first player to reach both those levels.

Aaron was the premier long-distance clouter not only of his era, but the best since Ruth. And when he finished the 1973 season, he had collected a career total of 713 home runs.

Hank had flown past the 700 mark, becoming only the second player in major league history to reach that plateau, when he socked one out in Atlanta against the Philadelphia Phillies' Ken Brett on July 21, 1973. Number 713 came in Atlanta on the next-to-last day of the season against the Houston Astros' Jerry Reuss.

The Braves' right fielder was considered a sure bet to break Ruth's record. That eventuality, however, was not universally applauded. Although he received some 930,000 pieces of mail in 1973 alone, much of it supportive, Aaron was also the recipient of many pieces of hate mail, mostly from brainless racists complaining about the color of his skin and the audacity of his threatening to break Ruth's record.

So venomous were some of the letters that Ruth's widow Claire felt compelled to make a public statement. "The Babe loved baseball so very much," she said. "I know he would have been pulling for Hank Aaron to break the record."

Despite the letters and the occasional threats to his life, Aaron went into the 1974 season fully confident of setting a new record. "The more they push me," he said of his detractors, "the more I want the record."

The Braves opened the season with a three-game series in Cincinnati. Hoping to save Aaron for a shot at the record before the Atlanta fans, Braves owner Bill Bartholomay planned to have Hank sit out the series with the Reds.

But Commissioner Bowie Kuhn learned about the plan, and after meeting with Bartholomay, he ordered the Braves to play Aaron in two of the three games in Cincinnati or suffer serious consequences. Hammerin' Hank was installed in the starting lineup. Predictably, in his first at-bat on his first swing in the first game of the series, after working the count to 3–1, he lined a Jack Billingham pitch into the left-field seats at Riverfront Stadium for a three-run homer.

The Braves eventually lost that game, 7–6, in 11 innings. Aaron failed to hit any more out; nor did he when he played again two days later, going 0-for-3 against Clay Kirby before being replaced in the late innings.

The next day—April 16—the Braves were back in Atlanta for their home opener against the Los Angeles Dodgers. By then, the eyes of the whole country were on Aaron. The vision was aided by the presence of thousands of newspaper and television reporters who had converged on Atlanta, as well as a national TV audience for the game.

It had rained during part of the afternoon, but 53,775 jammed the stands at Atlanta–Fulton County Stadium nonetheless. Launching the proceedings was a festive pregame show in which bands played, girls danced, a choir sang, fireworks were set off, and birds and 5,000 balloons were sent skyward. A 140-by-84-foot map of the United States was painted on the outfield grass. Aaron was paraded around the field through lines of majorettes, after which a film of his life flashed across the big screen in the outfield.

Governor Jimmy Carter of Georgia was there. So were dozens of movie stars and others from the entertainment world. A large contingent of the Aaron family was flown in from all around the country. Hank's father threw out the first ball.

After the speeches and the hoopla, the game finally began. Lefthander Al Downing was on the mound for the Dodgers. He walked Aaron on five pitches in the second inning, and the crowd booed lustily. Then Hank came to bat again in the fourth with two outs, Darrell Evans on first, and the Dodgers holding a 3–1 lead.

The first pitch was a ball in the dirt. The next was a fastball across the plate. Aaron with as powerul wrists as any hitter ever possessed, lashed his familiar whiplike swing at the ball, and in an instant it was flying over the outstretched glove of L.A. left fielder Bill Buckner and into the Atlanta bullpen in left-center where Braves reliever Tom House caught it.

As Aaron trotted calmly around the bases, pandemonium broke loose in the stadium. Dodger first baseman Steve Garvey and second baseman Davey Lopes shook his hand as he ran past them. Two Braves fans jumped out onto the field and joined Hank as he neared third where coach Jim Busby waited to greet him. By the time Hank reached home plate, his whole team, including members of the bullpen, were there to congratulate him, along with his father and mother, who gave him a bear hug.

Hank Aaron slammed his 715th home run in his 21st season in the major leagues.

The game was delayed for 10 minutes as Hank, his family, teammates, and fans celebrated the memorable event. There were a few speeches. It started to rain again, suddenly producing fears that the game was not yet official and could be erased if called off. Ironically, Kuhn was not in attendance, claiming he had a prior commitment. In his place, Kuhn's aide, ex-player Monte Irvin, was first booed, then cheered when he introduced Aaron.

Fighting back tears, Aaron said, "I just thank God it's finally over."

"When I hit it," Aaron said later, "it was truly one of the most remarkable evenings I've ever had in baseball. But the average person just can't realize what a nightmare this has been."

Downing was forthright about his role in the event. "It was a pitch he had to swing at," he said. "It was more toward the center of the plate than I wanted it to be. I was trying to keep the ball down and away, hoping maybe I could get him to hit a grounder. But it was a little bit higher than I wanted it, and Hank just dived into it and hit it out of the ballpark."

Aaron was 40 years old when he hit the shot that broke Ruth's record. Hank would have no more hits the rest of the game, which the Braves won, 7–4. Afterward, he was besieged by writers in the clubhouse.

"I'm not sure I hit the ball that hard," Aaron said. "Maybe I did, but I was so keyed up, I didn't feel it. But something carried the ball into the bullpen, and about the time I got to first base, I realized I was the all-time home run king of baseball.

"Now, I can consider myself one of the best. Maybe not the best because a lot of great ones have played the game. But I can fit in somewhere."

Indeed, he could. Aaron went on to scale even greater heights before his brilliant career came to an end after the 1976 season.

He finished the 1974 campaign with 20 home runs. Then, wishing to finish his career in the American League where he could perform as a designated hitter and not have to push his aging body across the outfield, he asked to be traded to the Milwaukee Brewers in the town where his career had started.

Aaron played two seasons with the Brewers, hitting 22 more home runs to bring his final total to 755. He ended his Hall of Fame career as not only the all-time leading home run hitter, but his 2,297 RBI, 6,856 total bases, and 1,477 extra-base hits also rank as the highest totals in baseball history.

Hank batted .305 during his 23 years. He ranks second on the all-time list in runs (2,174) and at-bats (12,364), and third in games (3,298) and hits (3,771).

Most significantly, he ranks first in hitting perhaps the most anxiously awaited home run ever hit.

Los Angeles	**AB**	**R**	**H**	**RBI**	**Atlanta**	**AB**	**R**	**H**	**RBI**
Lopes, 2b	2	1	0	0	Garr, rf, lf	3	0	0	1
Lacy, ph,2b	1	0	0	0	Lum, 1b	5	0	0	1
Buckner, lf	3	0	1	0	Evans, 3b	4	1	0	0
Wynn, cf	4	0	1	2	Aaron, rf	3	2	1	2
Ferguson, c	4	0	0	0	Office, cf	0	0	0	0
Crawford, rf	4	1	1	0	Baker, cf, rf	2	1	1	0
Cey, 3b	4	0	1	1	Johnson, 2b	3	1	1	0
Garvey, 1b	4	1	1	0	Foster, 2b	0	0	0	0
Russell, ss	4	0	1	0	Correll, c	4	1	0	0
Downing, p	1	1	1	1	Robinson, ss	0	0	0	0
Marshall, p	1	0	0	0	Tepedino, ph	0	0	0	1
Joshua, ph	1	0	0	0	Perez, ss	2	1	1	0
Hough, p	0	0	0	0	Reed, p	2	0	0	0
Mota, ph	1	0	0	0	Oates, ph	1	0	0	1
					Capra, p	0	0	0	0
Totals	34	4	7	4		29	7	4	6

Los Angeles	0	0	3	0	0	1	0	0	0	**4**
Atlanta	0	1	0	4	0	2	0	0	x	**7**

Los Angeles	**IP**	**H**	**R**	**ER**	**BB**	**SO**
Downing (L)	3*	2	5	2	4	2
Marshall	3	2	2	1	1	1
Hough	2	0	0	0	2	1
Atlanta	**IP**	**H**	**R**	**ER**	**BB**	**SO**
Reed (W)	6	7	4	4	1	4
Capra	3	0	0	0	1	6

*Pitched to four batters in fourth.

E–Buckner, Cey, Russell 2, Lopes, Ferguson. LOB–Los Angeles 5, Atlanta 7. 2B–Buckner, Russell, Wynn. HR–Aaron. SH–Garr. SF–Garr. WP–Reed. PB–Ferguson. T–2:27. A–53,775.

Frank Robinson

First Black Manager Has Smashing Debut

April 8, 1975 Municipal Stadium

As entertaining as they usually are, home runs are not always the whole show. Sometimes, they are exceeded by the event that surrounds them.

When that happens, though, the home run itself is sometimes elevated to a higher standing. By becoming part of a significant event, the home run becomes more important in its own right.

Such a distinction could certainly be claimed for the home run Frank Robinson hit in the 1975 season's opener for the Cleveland Indians at Municipal Stadium. The homer didn't win the game. It didn't fulfill any unique criteria. It merely made history because it was hit by the first African-American ever to manage a major league team in his first game at the helm. That alone made it a very special moment.

Robinson was hardly immune to hitting home runs, memorable or otherwise. During a brilliant 21-year playing career he would hit 586 of them, fourth-highest in big league history. He reached double figures in homers 19 times, and 11 times he hit 30 or more round-trippers, reaching a high of 49 in 1966 when he won his only home run title.

While winning National League Rookie of the Year honors in 1956, he tied a major league record for most homers by a freshman set in 1930 by

Wally Berger with 38. The mark would stand until Mark McGwire broke it in 1987.

On a path that led to the Hall of Fame, Robinson also became the first player ever to hit a ball completely out of Baltimore's Memorial Stadium when he rocketed a 451-foot shot over the outer wall in 1966. That year, while leading the Orioles to a four-game sweep of the heavily favored Los Angeles Dodgers in the World Series with key home runs that began the scoring in the first game and ended the scoring in the fourth game, Robby not only won the Triple Crown (.316–49–122), but he was also named Most Valuable Player in the American League. Combined with his MVP award when he sparked the Cincinnati Reds to the National League pennant in 1961, that accolade made him the only player who won MVP honors in both leagues.

Robinson joined a select group in 1971 when he hit two grand-slam homers in one game at RFK Stadium in Washington. Altogether, he hit eight homers in five trips to the World Series. By the time he retired as a player after the 1976 season, he had a .294 lifetime batting average with 2,943 hits and 1,812 RBI.

On October 3, 1974, after Cleveland had acquired him on waivers late in the season, Robinson and the Indians made history when Frank was signed to manage the club after it had a disappointing season under Ken Aspromonte. Robinson, who had prepared for this day by managing teams for six years in the Puerto Rican Winter League, had long campaigned for black managers in baseball.

Next to Jackie Robinson's entry into major league baseball with the Brooklyn Dodgers in 1947, Frank's signing was called the second most important step for blacks in a sport that had long been tainted by racial bias.

"If I had one wish I was sure would be granted," Robinson said at his introductory press conference, "it would be that Jackie Robinson could be here, seated alongside me today. This is the end of a long road, but the sacrifices were worthwhile to get here."

President Gerald Ford called to congratulate Robinson. He called the appointment "a tribute to you personally, to your athletic skills, and to your unsurpassed leadership."

While proud of his precedent-setting appointment, Robinson tried to keep race from being the dominant theme. "I am black, and I don't ignore the fact," he said. "But I'm not going out there as a black manager. I'm

Frank Robinson homered in his first at-bat as manager of the Indians.

going out there to manage. Judge me by how I do my job. If I don't do it, fire me."

Years later, Robinson discussed the historic signing at his induction into the Hall of Fame. "It was quite an honor and a thrill for me to open the door and be the first of my race to manage in the big leagues," he said. "Someone had to break through the door, and I was very proud that it was me."

Robinson was signed as a playing-manager by the same team that had signed Larry Doby in 1947 as the American League's first black player. Frank was 39 years old at the time, and was not expected to play regularly. The plan called for the hard-hitting righthanded batter to perform mostly as a designated hitter.

That is how Frank listed himself in the lineup when the Indians met the New York Yankees in the 1975 season's opener. He would bat second in the order.

Prior to the game, Indians general manager Phil Seghi, the man behind the signing of Frank as manager, called out to his new skipper. "Hey slugger," he yelled, "why don't you hit a homer the first time you go to the plate?"

Gaylord Perry was on the mound for the Indians. He and the always-outspoken Robinson had feuded during spring training, the pitcher criticizing the training program the new manager had mapped out. By the opener, though, the two had patched up their differences.

The Indians had won nine of 17 exhibition games. Robinson had batted only nine times, getting three hits. No one who followed baseball expected much from theTribe in 1975, but Robinson predicted a .500 finish.

Cleveland hardly had a power-packed lineup. It included some recognizable names in Robinson's old Orioles teammate Boog Powell as well as George Hendrick and Buddy Bell. Perry led the pitching staff.

After Jackie Robinson's widow, Rachel, threw out the first pitch, Perry, a future Hall of Fame righthander, set down the Yankees in the top of the first. Cleveland came to bat against George (Doc) Medich. Oscar Gamble, leading off for the Indians, was quickly retired. Robinson batted next.

Medich got two quick strikes on Frank. Then Robinson fouled off two pitches. Medich's next two offerings were wide for balls. Another foul followed before the Yankees righthander served up a slider that broke high over the plate for his eighth pitch to Robinson.

Frank took his usual big cut, and sent a blast high and deep to left. The ball landed in the stands for a home run, the first circuit clout ever hit by a black manager.

The crowd of 56,204, which had already given Frank one standing ovation when he was introduced before the game, stood and roared its approval as Robinson rounded the bases. One of the first to greet him in the Indians dugout was Perry. The two former adversaries fell into an emotional embrace.

"The first two strikes, I just couldn't pull the trigger," Robinson said later. "But then he came back with a sidearm motion. I saw him drop down, and boom. I just go blank after hitting, but when I got to third base, I thought to myself, 'Wow, will wonders never cease?' "

Unfortunately, the euphoria created by the homer was short-lived. The Yankees scored three runs in the top of the second. But Cleveland chipped away with single runs in the second and fourth. Then in the sixth, Powell, who had homered in the fourth, doubled home one run and Jack Brohamer singled in another to give the Indians and Perry enough for a 5–3 victory.

The dramatic home run, coming as it did in Robinson's first game as skipper, joined that historic event in headlines all over the country. It was duly noted as one of the crowning achievements of Robinson's brilliant career.

"Any home run is a thrill," Frank said. "But I've got to say, this one was a bigger thrill. It was the single most satisfying thing that ever happened to me other than winning. I feel better than I have after anything I've done in baseball."

Robinson had only a few more big moments with the bat. Seeing limited action through most of the season because of a shoulder injury, he came to the plate only 118 times and hit just nine home runs for the year while batting .237.

Nearly fulfilling their manager's prediction, Cleveland finished the season with a 79–80 record, good for fourth place in the AL West.

Robinson played even more sparingly in 1976 and collected just three home runs. He retired as a player at the end of the season after guiding the Indians to another fourth-place finish with an 81–78 record. The following season, he was relieved of his managerial duties in June with Cleveland in sixth place.

Frank went on to become the first black manager in the National League when he was hired by the San Francisco Giants in 1981. He piloted the Giants for three seasons, then skippered the Orioles in 1988 and 1989.

In nine seasons as a manager, Robinson compiled a 498–562 record, only once—in his final year—finishing as high as second place. It was not the record that mattered so much, though. It was the distinction of becoming the first black manager in major league history that really counted. And what made that extra special was the home run he hit in his very first game.

New York	**AB**	**R**	**H**	**RBI**	**Cleveland**	**AB**	**R**	**H**	**RBI**
Alomar, 2b	2	0	0	0	Gamble, lf	5	0	1	0
Johnson, ph	1	0	0	0	Robinson, dh	3	1	1	1
Stanley, 2b	0	0	0	0	Hendrick, cf	3	1	0	0
Piniella, lf	4	0	0	0	Spikes, rf	4	0	0	0
Bonds, cf	4	0	0	0	Powell, 1b	3	3	3	2
Blomberg, rf	4	1	2	0	Ellis, c	3	0	2	0
Nettles, 3b	4	1	1	0	Bell, 3b	4	0	0	0
Herrmann, dh	4	0	1	0	Brohamer, 2b	3	0	2	2
White, pr	0	0	0	0	Crosby, ss	4	0	1	0
Chambliss, 1b	4	1	3	2	Perry, p	0	0	0	0
Munson, c	4	0	2	1					
Mason, ss	3	0	0	0					
Medich, p	0	0	0	0					
May, p	0	0	0	0					
Lyle, p	0	0	0	0					
Totals	34	3	9	3		32	5	10	5

New York	0	3	0	0	0	0	0	0	0	**3**
Cleveland	1	1	0	1	0	2	0	0	x	**5**

New York	**IP**	**H**	**R**	**ER**	**BB**	**SO**
Medich (L)	5⅔	8	5	5	2	2
May	1⅓	0	0	0	1	1
Lyle	1	2	0	0	1	0
Cleveland	**IP**	**H**	**R**	**ER**	**BB**	**SO**
Perry (W)	9	9	3	3	1	6

E–Lyle. DP–Cleveland 1. LOB–New York 5, Cleveland 8. 2B–Chambliss. HR–Robinson, Powell. SB–Hendrick. SF–Brohamer. PB–Munson. T–2:43. A–56,204.

Carlton Fisk

Wave Goodbye to That One

October 21, 1975 Fenway Park

There is no such thing as an unexciting home run. Even the most mundane of four-baggers brings with it a certain dramatic flare, a spark accompanied by the ability to make the heart beat a little quicker.

Some home runs, of course, are more exciting than others. And then there are those that because of the situation are positively electrifying.

Into that highly select category fits the one that Carlton Fisk drove into the darkness in the wee hours of the morning of October 22, 1975, at Boston's Fenway Park in the sixth game of the World Series.

There are those who will tell you that Fisk's home run that night climaxed the most memorable game in World Series history. Those who say that would not be charged with lying. For the blast by the Boston Red Sox catcher did indeed conclude an absolutely remarkable game, the likes of which have not been seen either before or since.

No less an authority than the redoubtable Pete Rose, a participant in the game, verified that notion following Fisk's game-winning drive. "That was the most exciting game I ever played in," Rose said. "And I was on the losing team."

Fisk's homer, coming in the bottom of the 12th inning, gave the Red

Sox a 7–6 victory over Rose's Cincinnati Reds and sent a spine-tingling World Series into a pressure-packed seventh game. The blow not only continued what had been a remarkably exciting Series, but also capped an excruciatingly dramatic game during which a torrid battle had raged on the field.

"Rose came up to me in the 10th inning," Fisk recalled, "and said, 'This is some kind of game, isn't it?' And I said, 'Some kind of Series.' "

That it was. The Series pitted two of the premier teams in baseball. Boston had won the American League's East Division title by 4½ games over the Baltimore Orioles, then had swept the Oakland Athletics in three games in the League Championship Series. The Red Sox sweep had ended a three-year A's reign as American League champions while also finishing Oakland's hopes for a fourth straight World Series championship.

Cincinnati, meanwhile, had cruised home during the regular season with a 20-game lead and 108 wins, then swept the Pittsburgh Pirates in a three-game LCS to wins its third National League pennant in six years. In the midst of their Big Red Machine era, the Reds fielded a powerful team that featured Rose, Johnny Bench, Joe Morgan, Tony Perez, George Foster, and Ken Griffey.

There was no question that manager Sparky Anderson's Reds should be favored in the Series, especially with Boston rookie sensation Jim Rice sidelined for the event with an arm injury. But the Red Sox still had another rookie sensation in Fred Lynn, who doubled as the American League's Rookie of the Year and Most Valuable Player, plus aging slugger Carl Yastrzemski, as well as standouts Rico Petrocelli and Dwight Evans.

Fisk's playing time had been substantially reduced in 1975. The 1972 American League Rookie of the Year had missed much of the 1974 season, first with a groin injury, then with torn ligaments in his left knee after a collision at home with Cleveland's Leron Lee. After a winter of diligent rehab,he had suffered a fractured arm in the second game of spring training after getting hit with a pitch, and did not return to the lineup until June 23. Still he managed to hit .331 over the remainder of the season with 10 home runs and 52 RBI.

The 6–2, 200-pound backstop, a highly popular figure in Boston, especially because he came from nearby Vermont, was fully recovered, however, as postseason play began. His .417 average in the LCS helped to verify the point.

As Boston's cleanup hitter, Pudge, as he was called, was right in the middle of all the action in the early games of the World Series. Manager

Darrell Johnson's club won the opener, 6–0, on a five-hitter by Luis Tiant, but lost Game 2, 3–2, despite an RBI single by Fisk. Carlton had a solo homer in a 6–5 Red Sox loss in 10 innings in the third game, but more significantly was involved in a controversial play at the plate that led to the winning run. With Cesar Geronimo on first, pinch-hitter Ed Armbrister dropped a bunt, but he and Fisk became entangled in front of the plate. Off-balance, Fisk threw wildy into center field trying to get Geronimo at second. The Red Sox argued for an interference call, but their plea was ignored, and the Reds wound up with runners at second and third. Shortly afterward, Morgan singled home Geronimo with the winning run.

Boston won the fourth game, 5–4, behind Tiant. Don Gullett then won the fifth game for the Reds, 6–2, giving Cincinnati a 3–2 lead in the Series with the possible clincher moving back to Boston.

Three straight days of heavy rains, however, forced the delay of Game 6. Finally, the deluge stopped, and the two teams took the field on October 21 before a sellout crowd of 35,205. With rain-aided extra rest, Tiant took the mound against Gary Nolan.

Lynn's three-run homer vaulted Boston to a 3–0 lead in the first inning. In the fourth, Griffey tripled home two runs and scored on Bench's single to knot the score. Then the Reds went ahead in the seventh on Foster's two-run double before adding another run in the eighth on a homer by Geronimo.

Needing only six more outs and holding a three-run lead, the Reds appeared headed for certain victory. But with two on and two outs in the eighth, pinch-hitter Bernie Carbo, a former Red, touched Rawly Eastwick for a three-run homer, his second pinch-hit home run of the Series, and the game was tied at 6–6.

With the pressure mounting, Boston loaded the bases with none out in the ninth, but couldn't score as Foster caught Lynn's foul drive to left, then threw Denny Doyle out at the plate to squash the uprising. Evans followed with one of the great World Series catches in the 10th when he leaped above the wall in right field to make a one-handed grab to rob Morgan of a bid for a two-run homer.

It was Fisk's turn for some defensive heroics in the 11th. Carlton made a brilliant throw to second to force Rose on a sacrifice bunt attempt by Griffey that turned into a doubleplay. Pudge turned in another great defensive play in the 12th when he made a sprawling catch of Bench's pop foul with two Reds on base.

Carlton Fisk tried to will the ball fair in one of the most dramatic World Series games in history.

Cincinnati couldn't score in the 12th. Then, with the game passing the four-hour mark, Fisk came to bat leading off the bottom of the inning. Pat Darcy, the eighth Reds pitcher of the night, who was starting his third inning of relief, came in with a ball on his first pitch. The second pitch was a sinker, down and in. Fisk took a mighty swing, sending a high fly to deep left in the direction of Fenway Park's famed Green Monster.

The drive hugged the line. Would it be fair or foul? As the shot flew through the darkness, Fisk stood at the plate, trying to apply body English, desperately waving for the ball to go fair. The picture of Pudge trying to influence the path of the ball is one that baseball fans will never forget.

It seemed to take forever for the ball to land, but it finally came down, striking the foul pole on its descent, some 315 feet from home plate. Fisk leaped in the air, then strode deliriously around the bases as the Red Sox piled out of the dugout in celebration of their 7–6 victory.

"I knew it was going to go out," said Fisk. "It was just a question of its being fair or foul. I just stood there and watched, I didn't want to miss watching it go out.

"Then when it did, I made sure I touched every base," he added. "Even if I had to straight-arm people or knock them down, I made sure I touched every bit of white I saw out there.

"It was just a fantastic game. You're not exactly on top of the world when you're trailing a club like the Cincinnati Reds, 6–3, with four outs to go."

Even Anderson had to concede the point. "It was probably as good a ball game as I've ever seen," he said. "A great game in a great series."

Rick Wise, the fourth Boston pitcher, got the win in the game that finally ended at 12:34 A.M. But the euphoria in Boston was short-lived. The seventh game was anticlimactic. After a two-run homer by Perez put them ahead, the Reds triumphed, 4–3, on Morgan's RBI single in the ninth, giving Cincinnati its first World Series victory in 35 years.

There was no way the emotionally draining sixth game could be topped. It was certainly one of the most electrifying games in World Series history, climaxed by one of the most dramatic home runs ever hit.

Fisk went on to a long and splendid career in which he caught in more games than any other catcher in big league history. During a 24-year career that led to his induction into the Hall of Fame in 2000, he had a batting average of .269 and hit 376 home runs, including a record 351 for a catcher. For Fisk and all who saw it, though, the home run in the 1975 Series will never be forgotten.

Cincinnati	AB	R	H	RBI
Rose, 3b	5	1	2	0
Griffey, rf	5	2	2	2
Morgan, 2b	6	1	1	0
Bench, c	6	0	1	1
Perez, 1b	6	0	2	0
Foster, lf	6	0	2	2
Concepcion, ss	6	0	1	0
Geronimo, cf	6	1	2	1
Nolan, p	0	0	0	0
Chaney, ph	1	0	0	0
Norman, p	0	0	0	0
Billingham, p	0	0	0	0
Armbrister, ph	0	1	0	0
Carroll, p	0	0	0	0
Crowley, ph	1	0	1	0
Borbon, p	1	0	0	0
Eastwick, p	0	0	0	0
McEnaney, p	0	0	0	0
Driessen, ph	1	0	0	0
Darcy, p	0	0	0	0
Totals	50	6	14	6

Boston	AB	R	H	RBI
Cooper, 1b	5	0	0	0
Drago, p	0	0	0	0
Miller, ph	1	0	0	0
Wise, p	0	0	0	0
Doyle, 2b	5	0	1	0
Yastrzemski, lf-1b	6	1	3	0
Fisk, c	4	2	2	1
Lynn, cf	4	2	2	3
Petrocelli, 3b	4	1	0	0
Evans, rf	5	0	1	0
Burleson, ss	3	0	0	0
Tiant, p	2	0	0	0
Moret, p	0	0	0	0
Carbo, ph	2	1	1	3
Totals	41	7	10	7

Cincinnati	0	0	0	0	3	0	2	1	0	0	0	0	**6**
Boston	3	0	0	0	0	0	0	3	0	0	0	1	**7**

Cincinnati	IP	H	R	ER	BB	SO
Nolan	2	3	3	3	0	2
Norman	⅔	1	0	0	2	0
Billingham	1⅓	1	0	0	1	1
Carroll	1	1	0	0	0	0
Borbon	2*	1	2	2	2	1
Eastwick	1†	2	1	1	1	2
McEnaney	1	0	0	0	1	0
Darcy (L)	2‡	1	1	1	0	1
Boston	**IP**	**H**	**R**	**ER**	**BB**	**SO**
Tiant	7**	11	6	6	2	5
Moret	1	0	0	0	0	0
Drago	3	1	0	0	0	1
Wise (W)	1	2	0	0	0	1

*Pitched to two batters in eighth
†Pitched to two batters in ninth
‡Pitched to one batter in twelfth
**Pitched to one batter in eighth

E–Burleson. DP–Cincinnati 1, Boston 1. LOB–Cincinnati 11, Boston 9. 2B–Doyle, Evans,. Foster. 3B–Griffey. HR–Lynn, Geronimo, Carbo, Fisk. SB–Concepcion. SH–Tiant. HBP–By Drago (Rose). T–4:01. A–35,205.

Mike Schmidt

Leading a Remarkable Comeback

April 18, 1976 Wrigley Field

Most of the great hitters have memorable home runs on their résumés. Many have won crucial games. Others have won unusual games. A few that have been hit have been noteworthy strictly on their own merit.

When Mike Schmidt socked one into the bleachers on April 18, 1976, at Wrigley Field, it could be said that all three conditions applied. The homer won a crucial game for the Philadelphia Phillies. It certainly was an unusual game. And it put the future Hall of Fame third baseman into a special category among home run hitters.

By 1976, Schmidt was well established as a home run slugger. A rookie in 1973, he had won National League home run crowns in 1974 and 1975, and would win his third straight title in 1976. Eventually, Mike would capture seven home run titles and tie for an eighth, a total surpassed only by Babe Ruth.

A three-time Most Valuable Player, Schmidt homered in double figures in 13 seasons. By the time he retired in 1989, he had 548 home runs, more than any other third baseman in baseball history and the seventh-highest total of all time.

While Schmidt, who had a lifetime batting average of .267 in his 18 sea-

Mike Schmidt's fourth homer of the game gave the Phillies an 18–16 victory.

sons, was still ascending the ladder of a sterling career in his fourth big league season, the Phillies were finally emerging from the darkness of a long, dismal stretch. The club had last won a pennant in 1950. During most of the next 25 years, except for a brief interlude when they almost won a flag in 1964 before blowing a 6½-game lead with 12 games left to play, the Phils had been the picture of ineptitude.

But by the mid-1970s, the team, stacked with good, young players from a highly productive farm system, had finally become a contender again. And after a second-place finish in the NL East in 1975, the club had high hopes as it entered the 1976 campaign.

It was the country's bicentennial year, and a summer-long celebration was planned in the city of Philadelphia, the nation's birthplace. Nothing could be more apropos than a pennant drive by the resurgent Phillies.

For Schmidt, the '76 season began slowly. After the first four games, he was hitting just .167 and had already struck out nine times. The more he tried to break out of the slump, the more tense he became. "You've got to relax," advised Schmidt's close friend Dick Allen. "Have some fun. With all the talent you have, baseball ought to be fun. Enjoy it."

Schmidt was trying hard to heed Allen's advice as the Phillies met the Chicago Cubs on a cold, blustery afternoon at Wrigley Field. It was not much of a day for baseball. The wind blew strongly toward the left-field bleachers, and players wrapped themselves in layers of heavy clothing as they tried to keep warm.

To take some of the pressure off his young slugger, Phillies manager Danny Ozark had dropped Schmidt from third to sixth in the batting order, placing Greg Luzinski and Allen directly in front of him. Ozark sent ace lefthander Steve Carlton to the mound for the Phils.

In an attempt to change some things around himself, Schmidt abandoned his own bat and used a smaller one that belonged to Tony Taylor. Beneath his uniform, Mike put on a tattered T-shirt that was the property of Terry Harmon.

With Carlton on the mound, the Phillies always had at least a 75 percent chance of winning, but this was one of those days when odds meant nothing. The Cubs rocked the future Hall of Fame lefthander for seven runs in the second inning. Then they added five more in the third against relievers Ron Schueler and Gene Garber.

By the end of the third inning, the Cubs had a 12–1 lead. They stretched it to 13–2 after the fourth, and to all of the 28,287 in attendance, it appeared that the Phillies were dead.

The Phils, however, showed some signs of life in the fifth. "I believe the score was a blessing in disguise," said Schmidt, "because I think we all relaxed and decided to take some live batting practice."

Schmidt, who had flied out weakly to center in the second inning and singled sharply to left in the fourth, began the process when he jumped on a Rick Reuschel offering and pounded it over the left-field wall for a two-run homer. Two innings later, with Reuschel still on the mound, Mike clubbed another ball over the ivy-covered wall in left, this time with the bases empty. The blow came in the midst of a three-run inning in which the Phils cut their deficit to 13–7.

Suddenly, the Phillies were almost back in the game. They changed that "almost" to a "were" in the eighth with a five-run uprising that featured a three-run homer by Schmidt off Mike Garman. That made the score 13–12. With the wind blowing out, just about anything was possible, and the Phillies were exercizing that prerogative.

"I couldn't believe what was happening to me," Schmidt recalled. "But I decided to think about that later, and concentrate on winning. I was sure now that we were going to win."

Although Schmidt did not bat in the ninth, the Phillies scored three more runs with the help of a homer by Bob Boone to take a 15–13 lead in what was now one of the most improbable comebacks any major league baseball diamond had ever seen. The lead, however, was short-lived as the Cubs raged back with two runs of their own to send the game into extra innings.

The 10th inning couldn't have been any more dramatic. Allen led off with a walk off Darold Knowles. The Cubs then summoned Paul Reuschel, Rick's brother, to face Schmidt. Reuschel tried to run a fastball past him, but Schmidt was up to the challenge. He swung hard, and seconds later the ball sailed majestically into the bleachers in left-center.

It was Schmidt's fourth home run of the game. And it was the first time any National League player had hit four consecutive homers in a game since Boston's Bobby Lowe did it in 1894.

"The game was in the balance, but I wasn't thinking anything special when I went up there," Schmidt said later. "I was feeling good, and I was nice and relaxed. I was just trying to make contact, maybe get a single and move Dick to third where he could score on a fly ball. It's a lot easier to hit a home run when you're not trying to hit one.

"Reuschel tried to come inside on me," Schmidt added, "and I had what I thought was my best swing of the day."

The Phillies went on to score one more run in the inning. The Cubs added one in the bottom of the frame before Jim Lonborg, the eighth Phillies pitcher, got the last out, preserving the win for Tug McGraw and giving the Phils an 18–16 victory. There were 43 hits in the game, including nine home runs, with 13 different pitchers going to the mound.

It was a game that featured not only one of baseball's most incredible comebacks; it was also a game that served as a significant launching point for the Phillies. The amazing victory lit a fire under the team, and it went on to win 51 of its next 69 games en route to building a 15½-game lead in the NL East by late August.

Although the lead dropped to three games near the end of the season, the Phillies wound up winning the division title with a club-record 101 victories before losing in the League Championship Series in three games to the Cincinnati Reds.

The division crown was the first Phils title of any kind in 26 years, and it ushered in the team's finest era. Over an eight-year period between 1976 and 1983, the Phillies would win five division crowns, two National League pennants, and one World Series.

For Schmidt, it would be the greatest single game of his career. Mike finished with five hits while tying a club record with eight RBI. His four homers marked only the 10th time in baseball's long history that a player had hit that many homers in one game.

Schmidt went on to tie a major league record with 11 homers during the month of April. He concluded the season with 38 four-baggers to win his third straight home run crown.

Mike would have a number of other dramatic home runs during his career. Among them was his 10th-inning home run that gave the Phillies a 23–22 victory over the very same Cubs in 1979 in the highest-scoring one-run game and the highest-scoring extra-inning game in the 20th century. He also hit a two-run homer in the 11th inning of the next-to-last game of the 1980 season to give the Phillies a 6–4 win over the Montreal Expos and the NL East championship.

His best, though, came the day he hit four straight homers. Although nine others before him—and two others after him—have equaled that feat, no one's fourth homer was as dramatic or played as major a role in such a remarkable game as Schmidt's fourth drive over the wall. It was surely one of the most spectacular homers in one of the most amazing games.

Philadelphia	**AB**	**H**	**R**	**RBI**
Cash, 2b	6	1	2	2
Bowa, ss	6	3	3	1
Johnstone, rf	5	2	4	2
Luzinski, lf	5	0	1	1
Brown, lf	0	0	0	0
Allen, 1b	5	2	1	2
Schmidt, 3b	6	4	5	8
Maddox, cf	5	2	2	1
McCarver, ph	1	1	1	0
McGraw, p	0	0	0	0
Underwood, p	0	0	0	0
Lonborg, p	0	0	0	0
Boone, c	6	1	3	1
Carlton, p	1	0	0	0
Schueler, p	0	0	0	0
Garber, p	0	0	0	0
Hutton, ph	0	0	0	0
Reed, p	0	0	0	0
Martin, ph	1	0	0	0
Twitchell, p	0	0	0	0
Tolan, ph, cf	3	2	2	0
Totals	50	18	24	18

Chicago	**AB**	**R**	**H**	**RBI**
Monday, cf	6	3	4	4
Cardenal, lf	5	1	1	0
Summers, lf	0	0	0	0
Mitterwald, ph	1	0	0	0
Wallis, lf	1	0	0	0
Madlock, 3b	7	2	3	3
Morales, rf	5	2	1	0
Thornton, 1b	4	3	1	1
Trillo, 2b	5	0	2	3
Swisher, c	6	1	3	4
Rosello, ss	4	1	2	1
Kelleher, ss	2	0	1	0
R. Reuschel, p	1	2	0	0
Garman, p	0	0	0	0
Knowles, p	0	0	0	0
P. Reuschel, p	0	0	0	0
Schultz, p	0	0	0	0
Adams, ph	1	1	1	0
Totals	48	16	19	16

Philadelphia	0	1	0	1	2	0	3	5	3	3	**18**
Chicago	0	7	5	1	0	0	0	0	2	1	**16**

Philadelphia	IP	H	R	ER	BB	SO
Carlton	$1\frac{2}{3}$	7	7	7	2	1
Schueler	$\frac{2}{3}$	3	3	3	0	0
Garber	$\frac{2}{3}$	2	2	2	1	1
Reed	2	1	1	1	1	1
Twitchell	2	0	0	0	1	1
McGraw (W)	2	4	2	2	1	2
Underwood	$\frac{2}{3}$	2	1	1	0	1
Lonborg	$1\frac{1}{3}$	0	0	0	0	0
Chicago	**IP**	**H**	**R**	**ER**	**BB**	**SO**
R. Reuschel	7	14	7	7	1	4
Garman	$\frac{2}{3}$	4	5	5	1	1
Knowles (L)	$1\frac{1}{3}$	3	4	4	1	0
P. Reuschel	0	3	2	2	1	0
Schultz	1	0	0	0	0	0

E–None. DP–Philadelphia 1, Chiciago 1. LOB–Philadelphia 8, Chicago 12. 2B–Cardenal, Madlock 2, Thornton, Boone, Adams. 3B–Johnstone, Bowa. HR–Maddox, Swisher, Monday 2, Schmidt 4, Boone. SF–R. Reuschel, Johnstone. SFF–Luzinski, Cash. HBP–By Schueler (R. Reuschel), By Garber (Thornton). By Twitchell (Monday). B–Schultz. T–3:42. A–28,287.

Chris Chambliss

The Yankees Win the LCS

October 14, 1976 Yankee Stadium

What better time to hit a home run than to do it in a crucial game before the home fans? It is a feat that sends virtually everyone home happy except the losing team.

Sometimes, though, such an event can be carried to the extreme. That was certainly the case when Chris Chambliss struck a mighty blow for the New York Yankees on October 14, 1976, at Yankee Stadium.

If a poll were taken, it would probably be determined that Chambliss's home run was one of the most bizarre ever hit. Actually, it wasn't just because of the home run itself, but because of the events that followed it. Even under normal conditions, the situation would have begged for something out of the ordinary to happen. But these were no normal conditions.

The Yankees hadn't won an American League pennant since 1964. Years of frustration and disappointment had reduced the once-proud club to the level of an also-ran, and despite feverish attempts to elevate its place in the standings, it was simply unable to recapture the magic that had been so closely associated with the franchise.

The Yanks, however, had begun to pull out of the doldrums in the years immediately prior to 1976. The club finished a close second in 1974 and third in 1975. In 1976, with Billy Martin serving his first of five terms as manager, having been named to the post on August 2 the previous season, the club was once again a solid contender in the AL East.

The team had one other reason to feel good about itself. After playing at Shea Stadium for two years while Yankee Stadium was being renovated, the Yanks were finally returning home in 1976.

As the season began, the Yankees stormed out of the gate, built an early lead and by July were 15 games in front. The club went into a brief slump in early August, but by the end of the month had pushed its lead back to 11½ games. With attendance passing the two million mark for the first time since 1950, the Yanks roared home first, 10½ games ahead of the Baltimore Orioles.

To reach the World Series, though, the Yankees still had to get past the Kansas City Royals, an up-and-coming young team that had entered the league as an expansion franchise in 1969. The Royals were making their first playoff appearance after winning the AL West by just 2½ games over the former Kansas City A's, now based in Oakland.

League Championship Series were also relatively new, having just been initiated in major league baseball in 1969. At this point, the teams were still playing best-of-five sets.

The Yankees had a strong lineup that included Willie Randolph, Thurman Munson, Greg Nettles, Roy White, Mickey Rivers, and Lou Piniella. The first baseman was a steady, quiet, 28-year-old native of Dayton, Ohio, named Chris Chambliss, who had joined the Yanks in 1974 after a trade with the Cleveland Indians.

Chambliss, the American League's Rookie of the Year in 1971, had hit .304 in 1975 and .293 in 1976, a year in which he made his only appearance on his league's All-Star team. But until '76 when he hit 17 home runs, he had given little indication of being a consistent power hitter. Between 1971 and 1975, the 6–1, 195-pound lefthanded batter had hit just 41 homers.

New York won the first and third games of the series, 4–1 and 5–3, with Chambliss belting a two-run homer and driving in three runs in the latter. K.C. took the second and fourth games, 7–3 and 7–4. Thus the stage was set for the fifth and deciding game at Yankee Stadium. With a crowd of 56,821 jamming every corner of the stadium, Ed Figueroa took the mound for the Yankees, and Dennis Leonard toed the rubber for the Royals.

John Mayberry's two-run homer gave Kansas City the lead in the first inning, but the Yankees battled back and led 6–3 after six innings. The lead, however, disappeared in the eighth when George Brett socked a three-run homer to tie the score.

"The whole scene," Martin said later in a masterful piece of understatement, "came down to who would score one run first."

As the game reached the bottom of the ninth, no one had scored. Mark Littell, the fifth Royals pitcher of the game, was on the mound in his third inning of work as Chambliss stepped into the batter's box to lead off.

"Littell was a real good fastball, hard-slider pitcher," Chambliss recalled. "On the first pitch, he threw a high fastball, and I just swung at it. I happened to get it up in the air, but I didn't know it was gone because it really wasn't one of those bombs."

As it cleared the fence, Chambliss paused briefly to watch the flight of the ball while Royals right fielder Al Cowans made a desperation leap to catch it. The ball flew just over Cowan's glove and into the stands.

"I didn't go up thinking home run," Chambliss said afterward. "But I knew if he [Littell] gave me an inside pitch, I could pull it. And it was an inside pitch, and I pulled it. But I didn't get all of it. I waited a couple of seconds to watch it. Then I saw it go out, and I knew that was it. It was all over. We had the pennant."

The Yankees had the pennant, all right. It was their 30th flag. But for Chambliss, the night was far from over. He still had to get around the bases. That proved to be more difficult than hitting the home run.

"I saw Ellie Howard [Yankees first base coach] jumping and yelling," Chambliss said. "But from then on, I was just trying to hold onto my hat and fight people off so I could tag the bases."

Almost as soon as Chambliss reached first, fans started pouring out of the stands and onto the field. An army of fans caught up with Chris as he reached second and knocked him over. Chambliss got up and fought his way to third as a crowd of fans surrounded him.

"When I fell, I was really scared," Chambliss said. "I thought people might try to jump on me. I got up right away. Somebody tried to steal my helmet, so I took it off and put it under my arm. I felt like a football player. I used to be a running back. At that point, I couldn't think of anything else except to get to the dugout."

Third base coach Dick Howser tried to greet him. "It seemed like an

Chris Chambliss had to battle fans as he circled the bases at Yankee Stadium.

eternity for Chris to arrive," he said. "I was looking for him, but there were about 200 people between me and third base. For a while, he disappeared. I got a little scared. He could've been hurt. Eventually, he showed up, and he had a big, wide smile, so I knew everything was all right."

Chambliss struggled to find third base, but it apparently had been already stolen. He then rumbled down the third base line toward home plate. Such a huge crowd blocked his path, however, he never quite got there. After reaching the vicinity of home plate, Chambliss veered off away from the line, circled around the crowd, and headed toward the New York bench.

Chambliss battled through fans as he raced to the dugout, at one point bowling over a fan who stood in his way. Chris never stopped running until he got inside the Yankee clubhouse, where he was embraced by Figueroa.

Bedlam reigned in the clubhouse as players celebrated the Yankees' 7–6 victory and television crews and more than 100 reporters jammed into the room along with Yankees officials and others. Finally, Martin battled through the crowd to give Chambliss a message: he had to go back out onto the field and touch home plate to make his run official.

Escorted by two policemen in what had to be one of the strangest scenes in home run history, Chambliss had to fight through the frenzied crowd again to reach home plate. By the time he got there, the wild mob was ripping pieces of sod out of the field and even had pried up the plate. The damage was later assessed at $100,000.

Chambliss managed to get his foot in the vicinity of the dish, which by now was long gone. He then returned to the clubhouse where he and his teammates celebrated long into the early morning hours. Later, umpires told Chambliss he hadn't needed to try to find home plate.

"What a feeling,"Chambliss said. "This is number one in my life. There's never been anything like it before."

Chambliss wound up hitting .524 in the series with 11 hits, eight RBI, 20 total bases, and a .952 slugging average, all LCS records at the time.

Neither Chambliss nor the Yankees fared as well in their first trip to the World Series in 12 years. Chris hit a credible .313, but the New York ers were swept in four games by the Cincinnati Reds, then at the height of their power as the Big Red Machine.

Chambliss went on to a fine 17-year big league career in which he batted .279 with 185 home runs while playing in three more League Championship Series and two other World Series. Of all the batting he did, though, which included a key two-run homer that helped the Yankees defeat the Los Angeles Dodgers, 8–4, in the sixth and final game of the 1977 World Series, Chambliss never had a more unusual hit than the home run he blasted in the 1976 LCS. It was truly one of baseball's strangest home runs.

Kansas City	AB	R	H	RBI	New York	AB	R	H	RBI
Cowens, cf	4	1	1	0	Rivers, cf	5	3	4	0
Poquette, lf	3	0	0	0	White, lf	2	2	1	1
Wohlford, ph,lf	2	1	1	0	Munson, c	5	0	3	2
Brett, 3b	4	2	2	3	Chambliss, 1b	4	2	3	3
Mayberry, 1b	4	1	2	2	May, dh	4	0	0	0
McRae, rf	4	0	0	0	Alomar, pr,dh	0	0	0	0
Quirk, dh	4	0	0	0	Nettles, 3b	3	0	0	0
Rojas, 2b	4	1	1	0	Gamble, rf	2	0	0	0
Patek, ss	4	0	1	0	Randolph, 2b	3	0	0	0
Martinez, c	4	0	3	1	Stanley, ss	3	0	0	0
Leonard, p	0	0	0	0	Figueroa, p	0	0	0	0
Splittorf, p	0	0	0	0	Jackson, p	0	0	0	0
Pattin, p	0	0	0	0	Tidrow, p	0	0	0	0
Hassler, p	0	0	0	0					
Littell, p	0	0	0	0					
Totals	37	6	11	6		31	7	11	6

Kansas City	2	1	0	0	0	0	0	3	0	**6**
New York	2	0	2	0	0	2	0	0	1	**7**

Kansas City	IP	H	R	ER	BB	SO
Leonard	0*	3	2	2	0	0
Splittdorf	3⅔	3	2	2	3	1
Pattin	⅓	0	0	0	0	0
Hassler	2⅓	4	2	1	3	1
Littell (L)	1⅔†	1	1	1	0	1
New York	**IP**	**H**	**R**	**ER**	**BB**	**SO**
Figueroa	7‡	8	4	4	0	3
Jackson	1	2	2	2	0	1
Tidrow (W)	1	1	0	0	1	0

*Pitched to three batters in first
†Pitched to one batter in ninth
‡Pitched to one batter in eighth

E—Gamble, Brett. DP—New York 1. LOB—Kansas City 5, New York 9. 2B—Brett, Chambliss. 3B—Rivers. HR—Mayberry, Brett, Chambliss. SB—White, Rojas, Chambliss. SF—White, Gamble. SFF—Chambliss. T—3:13. A—56,821.

Reggie Jackson

Mr. October Goes to Work

October 18, 1977 Yankee Stadium

Home runs have a distinct way of elevating hitters to a higher level. A batter who hits home runs, or even one special four-bagger, is by virtue of his achievement placed on a pedestal that stands above his peers.

There is no finer example than Reggie Jackson, who on a single day in 1977 assured himself of the kind of notoriety reserved for special hitters. The fact that the feat occurred in a World Series at Yankee Stadium made it all the more prominent.

Three pitches, three different pitchers, three swings, and three home runs. An unimaginable feat, which rocketed the New York Yankees to the Series championship in the sixth game.

Jackson, of course, was a home run hitter of considerable note long before he earned himself the name Mr. October for his heavy hitting in the World Series. In 10 previous seasons—one in a late-season callup in the last year of the Kansas City A's, eight with the Oakland A's, and one with the Baltimore Orioles—the sturdy Jackson had reached double figures in home runs nine times, once winning and once tying for the home run title in the American League.

The lefthanded-hitting powerhouse had led Oakland to three pennants and three straight World Series victories from 1972 to 1974. Although injured and out of action in the '72 fall classic, he had hit merely two home runs in the following two Series.

Jackson came to the Yankees as a free agent before the 1977 season. It would be a rocky season as feuds raged throughout the Yankees from owner George Steinbrenner on down. Reggie, no stranger to controversy and a person who seldom held back his own opinions, battled much of the season, primarily with catcher Thurman Munson and manager Billy Martin. At one point, he and Martin almost came to blows in the dugout after the Yankees pilot accused Jackson of not trying hard enough for a fly ball.

Nevertheless, Jackson hit a solid .286 during the regular season with 32 homers and 110 RBI. And the Yankees registered 100 wins, won the division title on the next-to-last day of the season, and captured their second straight American League pennant after beating the Kansas City Royals, three games to two, in the League Championship Series.

Jackson, who seldom performed brilliantly in the LCS—in 11 years of LCS appearances during his career, he hit just .227 with six home runs—had managed only a .125 batting average with no home runs as the Yanks edged the Royals. He had even been benched in the final game of the series, although he delivered a key RBI pinch-hit single in the Yankees' 5–3 clincher.

In the World Series against the Los Angeles Dodgers, however, it was a different story.

The Dodgers under first-year manager Tom Lasorda were no pushovers. Led by 20-game winner Tommy John and heavy hitters Reggie Smith, Steve Garvey, Dusty Baker, and Ron Cey—each of whom had hit 30 or more homers during the season—the Dodgers had won 98 games and finished 10 games ahead of the defending World Champion Cincinnati Reds, who had swept the Yankees in four games the year before. L.A. then downed the Philadelphia Phillies in four games in the LCS.

The World Series opened at Yankee Stadium with the Bronx Bombers winning in 12 innings, 4–3, as Willie Randolph doubled and scored on a single by Paul Blair. Burt Hooton pitched a five-hitter to even the Series for the Dodgers with a 6–1 win in the second game.Then the Yanks came back with two straight wins at Dodger Stadium, gaining a 5–3 verdict in Game 3 on a seven-hitter by Mike Torrez and a 4–2 win in Game 4 behind Ron Guidry's four-hitter. Jackson, who had two hits in the first three games, unloaded a home run and a double in support of Guidry.

The Dodgers won the fifth game, 10–4, as Don Sutton pitched what would be the fourth of five complete games during the Series to get the win. Jackson, who had singled earlier, spanked a home run on Sutton's first pitch in his last at-bat of the game in the eighth inning.

Back at Yankee Stadium for the sixth game, the Yankees sent Torrez to the mound to try to wrap up the crown. The Dodgers countered with the righthanded Hooton.

Jackson, now batting .353 in the Series, drew a walk on four straight balls in his first trip to the plate in the second inning. By then, the Dodgers had jumped out to a 2–0 lead. But with Reggie scoring one of the runs, New York came back to gain a 2–2 tie in the second. The Dodgers then regained the lead with one run in the third. But that would change the next time Jackson came to bat.

After a leadoff single by Munson, Jackson came to bat again in the fourth. On Hooton's first offering, he drilled a hard liner over the wall in right field for his second home run in his last two official at-bats. Lou Piniella's sacrifice fly gave the Yanks another run later in the inning as the lead went to 5–3.

Reggie came to the plate again in the fifth inning with two outs. Mickey Rivers was on first after singling. Reliever Elias Sosa, in his second inning of work after replacing Hooton in the fourth, was on the mound for the Dodgers.

Jackson greeted the righthanded Sosa's first pitch to him with another line drive to deep right. It carried into the stands for Reggie's second homer of the game and third in the last three swings, and it gave the Yankees a 7–3 lead.

But the future Hall of Fame slugger wasn't done yet. He came to bat again in the eighth inning against knuckleballer Charlie Hough. Realizing what was happening, Yankees fans rose to their feet and screamed, "Reggie, Reggie, Reggie."

"It was a surreal moment," remembered Yanks second baseman Willie Randolph. "As a player, you're totally in awe of the situation. It was just so electric with the crowd roaring and Reggie stepping to the plate."

Hough's first pitch was a knuckleball that didn't knuckle too well. Jackson took a mighty swing, and the ball screeched off his bat, a tremendous smash that didn't stop until it had landed more than 450 feet away in the center-field bleachers.

Three swings against three different pitchers gave **Reggie Jackson** three home runs.

Yankee Stadium almost split at the seams as the crowd went wild. Three pitches, three swings, three home runs in one game, plus the one the previous day. Jackson had joined Babe Ruth as the only batters to hit three home runs in one World Series game. But no one, not even Ruth, who homered three times in a Series twice, had hit three in a row. Reggie's five homers also set a new Series record.

"It was," said Lasorda, who congratulated Jackson in the clubhouse afterward, "the greatest single performance I've ever seen."

Jackson's lusty hitting whipped the Yanks to an 8–4 win, a complete-game victory for Torrez, and the team's first world championship since 1962. And Reggie, finishing with a .450 batting average, was named the Series Most Valuable Player.

"When I hit the third one out," he said later, "I thought, 'I just won a new car for my sister.' " Cars were presented to the Series MVP in those days.

Randolph said that the third shot was the best. "The one before that was a bullet," he said. "But the third was a really good poke. It was some shot. Hitting three home runs like that was totally awesome."

Compared with Yankee deities Ruth, Lou Gehrig, and Joe DiMaggio, Jackson said he didn't consider himself a superstar. "It's nice to be compared with them. But I'm not that good," he added in a rare moment of modesty. "I had one game like those superstars had."

In that one game, though, Jackson had established himself as Mr. October, a name that would follow him long after his career ended in 1987. And his fall heroics would continue. The following year, Reggie added to his World Series laurels. He homered in the first game, then after a classic confrontation in the second game in which the Dodgers Bob Welch struck him out on a 3–2 pitch, Jackson came back to hit a two-run homer off Welch that helped the Yanks to a 7–2 win and victory in the World Series.

Reggie never had a bad World Series. He wound up hitting .357 with 10 home runs and 24 RBI in five Series. His .755 slugging percentage in 27 games was the highest ever registered.

He would go on to hit 563 homers, sixth highest in big league history. During a 21-year career, Jackson slammed more than 30 homers in a season seven times, reaching a high of 47 in 1969. Reggie had a lifetime batting average of .262 and won or shared four home run crowns. His 2,597 career strikeouts are a major league record.

Memorable home runs were numerous during Jackson's career. Of Reggie's many tape-measure clouts, the most noteworthy was certainly his 520-foot shot in the 1971 All-Star Game at Detroit's Tiger Stadium.

Nothing, though, could compare with the home run display Jackson put on in that 1977 World Series game. It was Mr. October's greatest show.

Los Angeles	**AB**	**R**	**H**	**RBI**	**New York**	**AB**	**R**	**H**	**RBI**
Lopes, 2b	4	0	1	0	Rivers, cf	4	0	2	0
Russell, ss	3	0	0	0	Randolph, 2b	4	1	0	0
Smith, rf	4	2	1	1	Munson, c	4	1	1	0
Cey, 3b	3	1	1	0	Jackson, rf	3	4	3	5
Garvey, 1b	4	1	2	2	Chambliss, 1b	4	2	2	2
Baker, lf	4	0	1	0	Nettles, 3b	4	0	0	0
Monday, cf	4	0	1	0	Piniella, lf	3	0	0	1
Yeager, c	3	0	1	0	Dent, ss	2	0	0	0
Davalillo, ph	1	0	1	1	Torrez, p	3	0	0	0
Hooton, p	2	0	0	0					
Sosa, p	0	0	0	0					
Rau, p	0	0	0	0					
Goodson, ph	1	0	0	0					
Hough, p	0	0	0	0					
Lacy, ph	1	0	0	0					
Totals	34	4	9	4		31	8	8	8

Los Angeles	2	0	1	0	0	0	0	0	1	**4**
New York	0	2	0	3	2	0	0	1	x	**8**

Los Angeles	**IP**	**H**	**R**	**ER**	**BB**	**SO**
Hooton (L)	3*	3	4	4	1	1
Sosa	1⅔	3	3	3	1	0
Rau	1⅓	0	0	0	0	1
Hough	2	2	1	1	0	3
New York	**IP**	**H**	**R**	**ER**	**BB**	**SO**
Torrez (W)	9	9	4	2	2	6

*Pitched to three batters in fourth

E–Dent. DP–New York 2, LOB–Los Angeles 5, New York 2, 2B–Chambliss. 3B–Garvey. HR–Chambliss, Smith, Jackson 3. SF–Piniella. PB–Munson. T–2:18. A–56,407.

Willie Stargell

Pops Wins One for "The Family"

October 17, 1979 Memorial Stadium

It's never too hard to spot a power hitter. He's usually a big guy. Large muscles bulge beneath his uniform. His shoulders are wide, and his arms are thick. He exudes strength. He looks like he could be a guy with the might to push over a small barn.

Nobody ever looked more like a power hitter than Willie Stargell. At 6–2, 225 pounds, he towered over mere ordinary ballplayers. And when he swung a bat, an act he performed with the utmost gusto, he resembled a giant swinging a child's toy.

Pops, as he was called in his later years as the leader of the Pittsburgh Pirates, was never shortchanged from getting his licks in. He made the most of every at-bat, much of the time to the chagrin of opposing pitchers. In fact, rare was the hurler who relished pitching against Stargell.

During a major league career that began late in 1962, covered 21 big league seasons, and culminated with his being elected to the Hall of Fame, numerous pitchers felt the sting of Stargell's big bat. Willie cracked 475 home runs while finishing with a career batting average of .282 with 2,232 hits and 1,540 RBI.

The seven-time All-Star selection led the National League in home runs twice, hitting a career-high 48 in 1971 and cracking 44 in 1973. Stargell struck out often, but he had 18 consecutive seasons in which he homered in double figures, and four times he slammed three four-baggers in a single game.

Stargell specialized in long-distance blows. He blasted four of the first five home runs hit into the upper deck at Pittsburgh's Three Rivers Stadium. Before that, he had hit 18 balls over the right-field roof at Forbes Field. Of the four balls hit out of Dodger Stadium in its first 39 years of existence, two were struck by Stargell. Willie was also the first batter to hit fair balls into the upper deck in both Busch Stadium in St. Louis and Veterans Stadium in Philadelphia.

Although it was not a tape-measure blast, surely Stargell's most memorable swat was the one he hit to win the 1979 World Series.

By that October 17 game at Memorial Stadium in Baltimore, Stargell had already enjoyed a remarkable season. Just three years short of retiring, the 38-year-old franchise leader in home runs had drilled 32 homers during the regular season with 82 RBI and a .281 batting average. The effort not only sparked the Pirates to the NL East title, which they clinched on the last day of the season with their 98th victory, but also earned Willie an unusual distinction. For the only time in major league history, the National League had co–Most Valuable Players, an award Stargell shared with Keith Hernandez of the St. Louis Cardinals.

Willie provided more than a big bat to the Bucs' attack. He was the captain and a popular clubhouse leader on a team that prided itself on its togetherness. Willie was a natural leader, and players both loved and respected him.

A popular song at the time was a number called "We Are Family" by a female vocal group known as Sister Sledge. The Pirates not only adopted the song, playing it at every opportunity, but widely proclaimed their own status as a "family." Much of that spirit was attributable to Stargell. Willie inspired as well as stablized the Pirates, and with his strong personality, he held the club together as a close-knit unit.

"We are just a ball club that is a family in the clubhouse," said Stargell, who awarded gold stars to players for good performances, the stars winding up on the Bucs' box-styled caps. "We aren't trying to be sassy or fancy."

After winning the division title by one game, the Pirates—with a heavy-hitting attack that featured not only Stargell, but also eventual four-time batting champion Bill Madlock, Dave Parker, and Bill Robinson—met the Cincinnati Reds in the NL playoffs. Stargell, appearing in the sixth and final LCS of his career, was the main show as manager Chuck Tanner's Pittsburgh club swept what just a few years earlier had been known as The Big Red Machine in three games.

In the first game, Willie's three-run homer in the 11th inning gave the Pirates a 5–2 victory. Stargell smacked a single and double in Game 2 as Pittsburgh won in 10 innings, 3–2. The Bucs triumphed in the deciding game, 7–1, with Bert Blyleven going the distance to get the win and Pops belting another home run and a two-run double. Stargell finished the series with six RBI and a .455 batting average, and was named the playoff's Most Valuable Player.

The lefthanded first baseman was back at it in the World Series against the Baltimore Orioles, piloted by Earl Weaver. The same teams had met in the 1971 Series with Pittsburgh winning in seven games. That time, although he had singled and scored the winning run on Jose Pagan's double in the eighth inning of his team's 2–1 victory in the seventh game, Stargell had contributed little else, managing only five hits and one RBI in 24 at-bats. But this time was different.

An eighth-inning home run by Willie was wasted in the first game as the Orioles triumphed, 5–4. After the Bucs captured a 3–2 decision in the second game with Stargell getting only a single, Willie smacked a single and double and scored twice in a third-game, 8–4 Baltimore victory. He then went 3-for-3 with a single, double, and home run in Game 4, but the Orioles again won, 9–6.

On the verge of elimination, the Pirates launched a comeback in the fifth game, winning, 7–1. Willie contributed a sacrifice fly in both that game and in the Bucs' 4–0 victory in Game 6, a combined shutout by John Candelaria and Kent Tekulve.

With the Series now pushed to a seventh game, the momentum had suddenly shifted to the Pirates. If they could win, they would become only the fourth team in baseball history to win a best-of-seven World Series after coming back from a three-games-to-one deficit.

Jim Bibby took the mound for the Pirates, facing the Orioles' Scott McGregor in the deciding game. A crowd of 53,733 jammed Baltimore's Memorial Stadium to watch the Birds go for their first world championship since 1970.

Baltimore drew first blood in the third inning on Rich Dauer's solo homer. McGregor then held the Pirates in check, and the Orioles clung to a 1–0 lead as the sixth inning began. Parker opened the frame with a groundout. Then Robinson stroked a hard shot that kissed off Orioles shortstop Kiko Garcia's glove and went into center for a single.

Stargell was next. Willie had already poled a single and double in his first two at-bats but had nothing to show for his work. Now McGregor, trying to work carefully, tried to slip a down and away slider past Stargell on the first pitch.

It was a good pitch, but not good enough. Stargell went after it and connected solidly. The ball didn't come down until it had crossed the right-field fence well over right fielder Ken Singleton's head and landed in the Pirates bullpen.

The shot unleashed a wild celebration on the Pirates bench. Pittsburgh suddenly led, 2–1, and there was no stopping the family now. The Bucs added two more runs in the ninth as Weaver sent five pitchers to the mound, and with Don Robinson, Grant Jackson, and Tekulve holding the Orioles to one hit over the final five innings, Pittsburgh waltzed off with a 4–1 victory.

"We scratched, we worked hard, we depended on each and every one of our 25 men," said Stargell, who added a late-inning double to finish the game with four hits. "And that is why we won the World Series. That's why we came from behind."

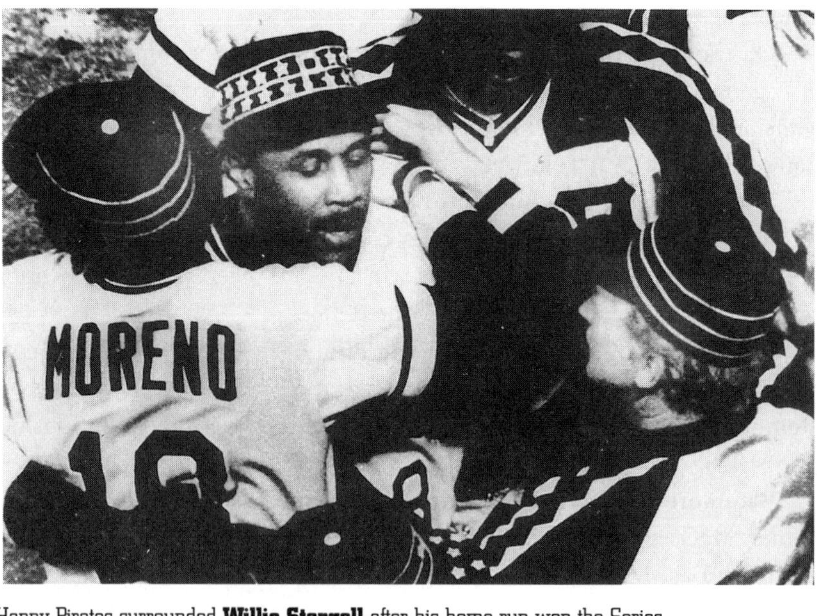

Happy Pirates surrounded **Willie Stargell** after his home run won the Series.

Stargell ended the Series with 12 hits, three of which were home runs, seven RBI, and a batting average of .400. Once again, he was named Most Valuable Player, making it three such awards for Willie in the same season. "I know just one person can receive the award," said Stargell afterward. "But if I could, I would divide it among the entire organization.

"To be part of this, the Good Man above has given us the right to shed tears at this point," he added. Stargell's teammates spoke glowingly of the season-long contribution he had made to the team. "The man is a legend," said Parker. "Right now, to me, he's like a god." For Stargell, it was the climax of a spectacular decade in which he had hit more home runs (296) during the regular season and driven in more runs (1,100) than any other major league player. In terms of clutch performances, though, nothing during Stargell's brilliant career equaled the home run he hit to win the 1979 World Series for the Pirates.

Pittsburgh	AB	R	H	RBI	Baltimore	AB	R	H	RBI
Moreno, cf	5	1	3	1	Bumbry, cf	3	0	0	0
Foli, ss	4	0	1	0	Garcia, ss	3	0	1	0
Parker, rf	4	0	0	0	Ayala, ph	0	0	0	0
B. Robinson, lf	4	1	1	1	Crowley, ph	1	0	0	0
Stargell, 1b	5	1	4	2	Stoddard, p	0	0	0	0
Madlock, 3b	3	0	0	0	Flanagan, p	0	0	0	0
Nicosia, c	4	0	0	0	Stanhouse, p	0	0	0	0
Garner, 2b	3	1	1	0	T. Martinez, p	0	0	0	0
Bibby, p	1	0	0	0	D. Martinez, p	0	0	0	0
Sanguillen, ph	1	0	0	0	Singleton, rf	3	0	0	0
D. Robinson, p	0	0	0	0	Murray, 1b	4	0	0	0
Jackson, p	1	0	0	0	Lowenstein, lf	2	0	0	0
Tekulve, p	1	0	0	0	Roenicke, ph, lf	2	0	0	0
					DeCinces, 3b	4	0	2	0
					Dempsey, c	3	0	0	0
					Kelly, ph	1	0	0	0
					Dauer, 2b	3	1	1	1
					McGregor, p	1	0	0	0
					May, ph	0	0	0	0
					Belanger, pr, ss	0	0	0	0
Totals	36	4	10	4		30	1	4	1

Pittsburgh	0 0 0 0 0 2 0 0 2 **4**
Baltimore	0 0 1 0 0 0 0 0 0 **1**

Pittsburgh	IP	H	R	ER	BB	SO
Bibby	4	3	1	1	0	3
D. Robinson	2/3	1	0	0	1	0
Jackson (W)	2 2/3	0	0	0	2	1
Tekulve	1 2/3	0	0	0	1	2

Baltimore	IP	H	R	ER	BB	SO
McGregor (L)	8	7	2	2	2	2
Stoddard	1/3	1	1	1	0	0
Flanagan	0*	1	1	1	0	0
Stanhouse	0*	1	0	0	0	0
T. Martinez	0*	0	0	0	0	0
D. Martinez	2/3	0	0	0	0	0

*Pitched to one batter in ninth

E–Garcia, Lowenstein. DP–Baltimore 1. LOB–Pittsburgh 10. Baltimore 6. 2B–Stargell 2, Garner. HR–Dauer, Stargell. SF–Foli. HBP–By T. Martinez (Parker), By D. Martinez (B. Robinson). T–2:54. A–53,733.

George Brett

Kansas City Finally Wins a Pennant

October 10, 1980 Yankee Stadium

Every once in a while a player performs so successfully during one particular season that he is forever linked to that year. Such was the case with George Brett in 1980.

Brett had banner years before that. And he had splendid seasons after that. But if there was one year during Brett's Hall of Fame career that above all others was associated with his name, it was that glorious 1980 season when the hard-hitting third baseman did just about everything except sell the hot dogs.

For starters, Brett hit 24 home runs and drove in a career-high 118 runs during the regular season. He led the American League with a .664 slugging average. He hit 33 doubles and scored 87 runs. And he was named the league's Most Valuable Player.

More significantly, Brett ran away with the batting title, parlaying a 30-game hitting streak into a remarkable .390 batting average. It was the highest average since Ted Williams hit .406 in 1941.

Then with one final piece of heroics, Brett capped his dazzling season with the biggest home run in Kansas City Royals history. The blow landed the Royals in the World Series for the first time after three futile attempts.

George Brett hit the biggest home run in Kansas City Royals history.

The lefthanded-swinging Brett was one of the great players of his era. During a glittering 21-year big league career, he won three batting crowns, the only player to win one in three different decades. He was named to 13 All-Star teams. And he hit above .300 11 times, finishing his career with a batting average of .305 with 3,154 hits.

The apex of Brett's career, though, was in 1980. That season, more than any other, belonged to George.

He flirted with a .400 batting average through much of the season, even going above that exalted mark from mid-August to mid-September when it seemed as though Williams' iron grip on a .400 season would finally be challenged. All the while, Kansas City was dominating the AL West with a heavy-hitting lineup that wound up batting 19 points higher than the next-closest American League team.

The Royals won the AL West title by 14 games to advance to the League Championship Series against the New York Yankees, winners of 103 games during the regular season and owners of the best record in the major leagues. The best-of-five series pitted old, familiar rivals. The Royals and Yankees had met in the playoffs in 1976, 1977, and 1978. New York had won the first two meetings, three games to two, and the third, three games to one. "We hated each other," Brett said. "The Royals and Yankees hated each other. It was a great rivalry. We had fun, and we had physical games."

Brett was no stranger to heroics in those series. He had hit four home runs in them, including a three-run homer in the eighth inning of the fifth game of the 1976 series that tied the game at 6–6 and set the stage for Chris Chambliss's memorable homer. He also slammed three dingers in a 6–5 Yankees win in the third game of the 1978 LCS.

But victory continued to elude the Royals, and as they entered the 1980 LCS, they were once again underdogs to the Yankees, winners of 28 of their final 37 regular-season games. The Yanks had won two World Series since 1976. "Past history doesn't mean a thing," rumbled Brett before the Series got under way.

Brett, whose brother Ken had set a Philadelphia Phillies record in 1973 with home runs in four straight games in which he pitched, homered to help the Royals to a 7–2 win in the first game. The Royals then captured the second test, 3–2, with the help of Brett's defense. He threw out Willie Randolph at the plate trying to score the tying run on Bob Watson's eighth-inning double.

The series then moved to New York for the third game. A 32-minute rain delay interrupted play in the early going before the Royals took a 1–0 lead on Frank White's home run in the fifth. But the Yankees came back with two runs in the sixth. Then it was the Royals turn to step forward.

With two outs in the seventh, Willie Wilson doubled to right. The hit kayoed the Yanks' starter, 22-game winner Tommy John. He was replaced by the intimidating fireballer Goose Gossage.

Gossage, one of the premier relievers of his era, had given up only five home runs all season. He immediately gave up an infield hit to U. L. Washington, who ran hard to beat out a bouncer up the middle. That brought up Brett, who hadn't had a hit in his last seven trips to the plate.

"When Gossage is pitching," Brett said later, "you don't look for a change-up. I'd been swinging bad all series, but I think I can hit speed as good as anybody.

"I just wanted to pull the ball. I knew it was only 310 feet down the line, so it didn't take too much to get it into the seats. I wanted to pull the ball and get it up in the air."

It was a classic case of power versus power. The first pitch by Gossage was the fastball Brett was looking for. George swung, and what left his bat was a high, towering fly to deep right. The ball landed five rows into the third deck of Yankee Stadium, an estimated 450 feet from home plate. For Brett, it was only his third hit of the series.

Wilson and Washington danced home ahead of Brett, giving the Royals a 4–2 lead. Gossage, pitching for the first time in five days, looked dejectedly down at the ground. "I feel I'm the best around, and he's the best around," Gossage said. "He beat me this time. It just came at an awful time. I feel like we let down the [Yankee] tradition. That really hurts."

"I knew it was out," said Yankees manager Dick Howser. "I didn't even get up. I just started thinking of who was going to pitch the next inning."

The Yankees still had three more at-bats. But Royals relief ace Dan Quisenberry, who had replaced Paul Splittorff in the sixth inning, held the Yanks the rest of the way. Quisenberry, who tied Gossage in 1980 for the league lead in saves with 33, had to overcome Watson's leadoff triple in the seventh and a one-out, bases-loaded jam in the eighth. Washington made a sparkling catch and turned it into a doubleplay to help preserve the victory.

Quisenberry retired the side in order in the ninth, and as 56,588 watched, Kansas City walked off with a sweep and its first pennant in 12 years in the league.

"We had gone through such a struggle with Oakland and New York, and to finally beat them was very exciting," recalled Hal McRae, who was in the on-deck circle when Brett cracked his homer. "It seemed like those two clubs always gave us trouble. We were very happy to beat them and to earn a chance, finally, to get to the World Series."

For Brett, the home run meant even more than becoming the first player since 1941 to hit .400 would have meant, had he done that. "I went over .400 [during the season], and hitting .400 was one of my priorities," said Brett. "I wanted it, but not as bad as I wanted this. I've respected the Yankees since I was a little boy. For us to beat New York is the ultimate."

Brett paid tribute to Washington, whose hustle down the line on an infield bouncer that Randolph fielded behind second base kept the Royals alive in the seventh inning. "He busted his butt," George said. "If he hadn't busted his butt, the inning would've been over and the best I could have done leading off the eighth was a one-run homer."

Although they finally won a pennant, the Royals' luck had run out. They lost in six games to the Phillies in the World Series. Brett hit .375 in the Series.

George would have other memorable home runs. One was his infamous "pine tar" homer in 1983 when an apparent two-run homer, which gave the Royals a 5–4 lead in the ninth inning in a game at Yankee Stadium, was ruled illegal (but later reinstated) because Brett was using a bat that had pine tar too far up on the handle. Ironically, the 400-foot blast was also against Gossage.

"George was one of the few guys who could hit Gossage," McRae said. "He [Gossage] usually shut the rest of us down."

Brett also hit three homers in the Royals' 1985 LCS win over the Toronto Blue Jays, two of which came during a 4-for-4, 11-total-bases outburst in KC's 6–5 victory in the third game.

But of all his homers, none was as memorable as the one Brett hit in 1980 to win a pennant for the Kansas City Royals. It came during a season that like no other belonged to Brett.

Kansas City	**AB**	**R**	**H**	**RBI**	**New York**	**AB**	**R**	**H**	**RBI**
Wilson, lf	5	1	2	0	Randolph, 2b	4	0	1	0
Washington, ss	4	1	2	0	Dent, ss	4	0	0	0
Brett, 3b	4	1	1	3	Watson, 1b	4	0	3	0
McRae, dh	4	0	2	0	Jackson, rf	3	1	1	0
Otis, cf	4	0	1	0	Soderholm, dh	2	0	0	0
Aikens, 1b	4	0	3	0	Gamble, ph, dh	1	1	1	0
Porter, c	3	0	0	0	Cerone, c	4	0	1	1
Hurdle, rf	2	0	0	0	Piniella, lf	2	0	0	0
Wathan, ph, rf	2	0	0	0	Spencer, ph	1	0	0	0
White, 2b	4	1	1	1	Lefebvre, lf	0	0	0	0
Splittorff, p	0	0	0	0	Rodriguez, 3b	2	0	1	0
Quisenberry, p	0	0	0	0	Nettles, ph, 3b	2	0	0	0
					Brown, cf	4	0	0	0
					John, p	0	0	0	0
					Gossage, p	0	0	0	0
					Underwood	0	0	0	0
Totals	36	4	12	4		33	2	8	1

Kansas City	0 0 0 0 1 0 3 0 0 **4**
New York	0 0 0 0 0 2 0 0 0 **2**

Kansas City	**IP**	**H**	**R**	**ER**	**BB**	**SO**
Splittorff	5⅓	5	1	1	2	3
Quisenberry (W)	3⅔	3	1	0	2	1

New York	**IP**	**H**	**R**	**ER**	**RB**	**SO**
John	6⅔	8	2	2	1	3
Gossage (L)	⅓	3	3	3	0	0
Underwood	2	1	0	0	0	1

E–White. DP–Kansas City 2, New York 1. LOB–Kansas City 6, New York 8. 2B–Watson, Jackson, Wilson. 3B–Watson. HR–White, Brett. WP–John. B–Splittorff. T–2:59. A–56,588.

Jack Clark

A New Hero Joins Cardinals Legends

October 16, 1985 Dodger Stadium

One of the subtle beauties of a home run is its spontaneity. No one knows for sure when one is going to be hit. It just happens. One instant there's a pitch. The next instant a ball is flying over the fence.

You can't prepare for a home run. You can't predict when one will be hit. And there is certainly no way to anticipate whose home run might make the difference in a big game.

There was certainly no way to figure Jack Clark would be the hero as the Los Angeles Dodgers and St. Louis Cardinals met in the sixth game of the National League Championship Series on October 16, 1985, at Dodger Stadium. After all, Clark had been so bothered by a rib-cage injury that he had hardly played since August 23. He had only one home run since then.

Clark, of course, was a potent home run threat when he was healthy. In a career that had begun in 1975 with the San Francisco Giants, he had by the time he came to the Cardinals in 1985 already smacked 163 home runs with eight seasons in double figures. And by the time his career ended in 1992, he had amassed 340 round-trippers.

Clark, who hit .267 during his 18-year career, was surely a hitter to be reckoned with. That's why the Cardinals sent four players to the Giants to

Ninth-inning home run by **Jack Clark** led the Cardinals into the World Series.

get him, hoping he'd be a major source of power in a St. Louis lineup bulging with speedy singles hitters.

The big righthanded-hitting outfielder/first baseman, who was nicknamed "The Ripper," lived up to his promise. He hit 22 homers, drove in 87 runs, and hit .281 in his first season with the Cardinals. But the rib-cage injury hampered his swing considerably in the waning stages of the season, and he missed 40 games in the last six weeks.

Nonetheless, with Willie McGee winning the NL batting title with a .353 average, Rookie of the Year Vince Coleman leading the league with 110 stolen bases, Ozzie Smith playing shortstop like no other has ever played it, and Tommy Herr, Terry Pendleton, and Andy Van Slyke providing solid, steady performances, the Cardinals won 101 games during the regular season and captured the division title by three games over the New

York Mets. Joaquin Andujar and John Tudor each won 21, and Danny Cox copped 18 wins to lead a splendid pitching staff.

The Cardinals, a team that relied almost entirely on speed, defense, and pitching—the club hit just 87 home runs all season—then moved into the LCS where they faced the Dodgers, winners of 95 games and the West Division title by 5½ games. It would be another in a long line of showdown series between the two bitter National League rivals.

Fernando Valenzuela and Orel Hershiser, winners of a combined 36 games during the regular season, bested Tudor and Andujar, 4–1 and 8–2, respectively, in the first two games of the playoffs at Dodger Stadium. Moving to Busch Stadium, the Cardinals regained the upper hand with three straight wins, as Cox and Tudor got the first two wins by 4–2 and 12–2 scores. Clark, who had just two singles in the first three games, slammed three hits and scored three runs in Game 4.

Ozzie Smith, who would become the series MVP, provided the heroics in Game 5 with a stunning home run in the bottom of the ninth inning that gave St. Louis a 3–2 victory. It was only the 14th major league home run of the light-hitting Smith's career, and his first batting lefthanded after more than 4,000 at-bats.

Smith's dramatic blast set the stage for the sixth game as the best-of-seven series returned to Los Angeles. With Andujar facing Hershiser, a crowd of 55,208 packed Dodger Stadium to see if the Dodgers could prolong the series.

It looked like they would as the Dodgers jumped out to a 2–0 lead, then upped the count to 4–1 with the help of an RBI single and solo home run by Bill Madlock. But the Cards weren't about to roll over. They knocked out Hershiser with a three-run seventh, tying the score on an RBI triple by Smith off reliever Tom Niedenfuer.

Ironically, Niedenfuer, a hard-throwing righthander who had collected seven wins and 19 saves during the season, was the same pitcher who had given up Smith's home run in Game 5. The irony, however, still had another chapter.

After Smith's triple, Niedenfuer escaped further damage by issuing an intentional walk to Herr, then striking out Clark and Van Slyke. "It was like a slap in the face," said Clark later about the intentional walk.

With the score deadlocked at 4–4, Mike Marshall put the Dodgers back in front and seemingly assured the series of reaching the seventh game with a solo homer off Todd Worrell in the bottom of the eighth. St. Louis had just one more chance.

With one out in the ninth, McGee singled and stole second. Smith walked, then both runners advanced one base on Herr's easy ground out to first. The Cardinals were down to their final out with Clark coming to the plate.

Controversy waited in the wings. Many observers figured that with first base open, Clark would be given an intentional pass, even though Niedenfuer had struck him out two innings earlier. It seemed to make more sense to face Van Slyke, who had just one hit in the entire series, than the ever-dangerous Clark.

"When you manage a baseball team, you only have one guess," said manager Whitey Herzog. "I'm not second-guessing him [Dodgers skipper Tom Lasorda], but I thought they'd probably walk him."

They didn't. And Clark jumped on Niedenfuer's first pitch, a fastball down and in, and sent it crashing 20 rows up in the left-center-field bleachers, some 450 feet from home plate. The blast gave the Cardinals a 7–5 lead.

As soon as the ball was hit, Clark looked over toward the Cardinals bench. "I knew it was going to be a home run," he said. "That was for my teammates.

"It was power against power," Clark added. "When I walked up to the plate, I wasn't trying to hit a home run. That's the same pitcher who got me out. He's capable of doing it again. I was just trying to hit a single, and knock in the tying run. I was looking for a fastball, and I got it."

St. Louis reliever Ken Dayley set the Dodgers down in order in the bottom of the ninth to preserve the decision for Worrell. And the Cardinals skipped into the clubhouse with a 7–5 victory and their 14th trip to the World Series.

Lasorda defended his decision to pitch to Clark, saying he didn't want the righthanded Niedenfuer pitching to the lefthanded Van Slyke. He also said he didn't want to risk loading the bases so that a walk could force home a run. After the game, he apologized to his players.

"If I could only relive that inning," he added. "I wanted him to make Clark go for a bad pitch, go to his weakness. Instead, he put a fastball down the middle."

Said Niedenfuer: "It was the manager's decision [to pitch to Clark]. I had struck him out on sliders before, and I figured he'd be looking for sliders again. I tried to sneak a fastball by him and get ahead in the count, but it didn't get there.

"The only way that shot would have stayed in the ballpark," Niedenfuer added, "was if it hit the Goodyear blimp."

Clark's smash not only propelled the Cardinals into the World Series. It was immediately hailed as one of the biggest—if not the biggest—home runs in Cardinals history.

"It certainly was the greatest home run of my life," Clark said. "I've been in clutch situations in the past, so I felt prepared. I decided I was going to take three good swings. I saw the ball real well. I saw the rotation on the seams. I thought they might try to work around me, maybe throw some pitches away, but not a fastball in on me.

"I'm not the hero," he insisted. "It [the win] was special for me, but more special for them [his teammates]."

Clark wound up with a .381 batting average in the series. Neither he nor the Cardinals fared as well, however, in the World Series.

Facing the Kansas City Royals in the first all-Missouri Series since 1944, the Cardinals played without Coleman, who suffered a freak injury before the first game when a Busch Stadium tarpaulin accidentally rolled over his leg. Umpire Dan Denkinger's missed call at first base in the sixth game added to the confusion as the Cardinals lost the Series in seven games. Clark had just six hits in the Series, including four singles and two doubles.

Torn thumb ligaments cost Clark much of the 1986 season before he came back to hit a career-high 35 homers in his final season in St. Louis. Jack wound up with a total of 66 homers in a Cardinals uniform. One in particular made a very special mark in the St. Louis registry of memorable hits.

St. Louis	AB	R	H	RBI	Los Angeles	AB	R	H	RBI
McGee, cf	5	2	3	2	Duncan, ss	5	2	3	1
Smith, ss	4	1	2	1	Landreaux, cf	4	0	0	0
Herr, 2b	3	0	1	1	Cabell, ph	1	0	0	0
Clark, 1b	5	1	2	3	Guerrero, lf	3	0	0	1
Van Slyke, rf	5	0	0	0	Madlock, 3b	4	1	2	2
Pendleton, 3b	4	0	0	0	Anderson, 3b	0	0	0	0
Porter, c	4	1	2	0	Marshall, rf	4	1	1	1
Landrum, lf	4	1	1	0	Scioscia, c	3	0	1	0
Andujar, p	2	1	1	0	Brock, 1b	2	1	0	0
Braun, ph	1	0	0	0	Sax, 2b	4	0	0	0
Worrell, p	0	0	0	0	Hershiser, p	3	0	1	0
Cedeno, ph	1	0	0	0	Niedenfuer, p	1	0	0	0
Dayley, p	0	0	0	0					
Totals	38	7	12	7		34	5	8	5

St. Louis	0	0	1	0	0	0	3	0	3	**7**
Los Angeles	1	1	0	0	2	0	0	1	0	**5**

St. Louis	IP	H	R	ER	BB	SO
Andujar	6	6	4	2	2	3
Worrell (W)	2	2	1	1	2	2
Dayley	1	0	0	0	0	2
Los Angeles	**IP**	**H**	**R**	**ER**	**BB**	**SO**
Hershiser	6⅓	9	4	4	1	1
Niedenfuer (L)	2⅔	3	3	3	2	3

E–Andujar. DP–St. Louis 1. LOB–St. Louis 7, Los Angeles 7. 2B–Duncan, Andujar. 3B–Smith, Duncan. HR–Madlock, Marshall, Clark. SB–Duncan, McGee. SF–Guerrero. T–3:32. A–55,208.

Kirk Gibson

Hobbled Hitter Leads Dodgers to Victory

October 15, 1988 Dodger Stadium

In the minds of those who see them, home runs have different levels of staying power. Some are hit and quickly forgotten. Others linger for a while, but eventually the mind discards them. Then there are those special few which etch an indelible image that lasts a lifetime.

Those who saw Kirk Gibson's home run in the first game of the 1988 World Series know what that is. Gibson's heroics have carved an unforgettable niche in their minds, at the same time forming one of the most memorable sights ever witnessed on a baseball diamond.

Years later, the picture lingers. The grizzled Gibson, barely able to walk, hobbles to the plate as a pinch-hitter in the bottom of the ninth inning. Two outs, one man on base. Gibson's Los Angeles Dodgers trail the heavily favored Oakland Athletics 4–3. Relief ace Dennis Eckersley is on the mound for the A's.

With both legs wracked with injuries, Gibson can hardly swing. He flails feebly at Eckersley's pitches. Then, with the count at 3–2, he summons his deepest reserves, pounces on an outside slider, and drives it over the right-field fence.

Gibson, named the National League's Most Valuable Player in 1988

Kirk Gibson chugged around the bases after dramatic ninth-inning pinch-hit homer.

after hitting .290 with 25 home runs, lurches out of the box, stumbles, then chugs triumphantly around the bases, cranking his arms as he goes. The blast gives the Dodgers a 5–4 victory, and although Gibson will not play again in the Series, it provides the momentum to send L.A. to the championship in five games.

Surely, few homers—World Series or otherwise—equal Gibson's for drama or for the sight they created. It was one of the great scenes of all time.

It almost didn't happen. After a fine career with the Detroit Tigers, the muscular outfielder had come to the Dodgers as a free agent before the 1988 season. The Dodgers weren't supposed to be a strong contender that year, but they played surprisingly well most of the season, and finished the regular season in first place in the National League's West Division, seven games ahead of the Cincinnati Reds.

L.A. continued to amaze the experts as it beat the favored New York Mets in seven games in the League Championship Series. Gibson, who hit just .154 during the series, had won the fourth game with an 11th-inning home run, giving the Dodgers a 5–4 victory. His three-run homer in the fifth inning of Game 5 was the big blow in a 7–4 Dodger win that vaulted L.A. to a 3–2 lead in the series.

But in Game 6 at Dodger Stadium, the former Michigan State wide receiver—who had shunned college baseball until the coach, ex–major leaguer Danny Litwhiler, had finally persuaded him to come out in his senior year—pulled a hamstring in his left leg while sliding into second with a stolen base. If that wasn't bad enough, Gibson then hurt his other leg during the Dodgers clinching 6–0 victory in the seventh game when he strained a ligament in his right knee as he slid into second while trying to break up a double play.

Gibson spent the next two days at home trying to get his badly damaged legs back into playing shape. But it was an exercise in futility. He could barely walk. "I couldn't even do a little jog in my living room," he said.

When the World Series opened two days after the Mets series ended, Gibson was in no shape to play. That spelled bad news for the Dodgers as they went up against the powerful A's.

Oakland featured a lineup built around the Bash Brothers, Mark McGwire and Jose Canseco, and speed demon Rickey Henderson. The A's had won 104 games during the regular season, winning the flag by 13 games before sweeping the Boston Red Sox in four straight in the LCS. There seemed little chance that manager Tommy Lasorda's Dodgers, a team heavily stacked with journeymen and with few star players, could compete on the same level as the haughty Athletics.

That view was borne out as the Series began. In Game 1, the Dodgers jumped out to a 2–0 lead in the first inning as Mickey Hatcher touched A's ace Dave Stewart for a two-run homer. The lead, however, didn't last. The A's came back in the top of the second with four runs as Canseco drilled the first grand slam of his career off L.A. starter Tim Belcher.

The Dodgers added a lone run in the sixth on an RBI single by Mike Scioscia, but they still trailed, 4–3, as the game went to the bottom of the ninth.

Gibson had spent almost the entire game in the Dodgers clubhouse, applying an ice pack to his ailing parts. With the game being played in L.A., there was no designated hitter in use, and Kirk had little chance of seeing any action.

"He can't do it. He just can't do it," Lasorda had said before the game. The pronouncement seemed not to be lacking in accuracy.

But late in the game, Gibson decided he might be able to pinch-hit. His knee, especially, was throbbing, but when he removed the ice pack, he discovered the knee would stay numb for a few minutes, long enough to make a quick plate appearance.

"I watched the whole game from the trainer's room. Then I decided it was time to give it a try," said Gibson, a .268 hitter with 255 home runs during a 17-year career in the major leagues.

Kirk got one of the Dodgers batboys to accompany him to the team's batting cage beneath the stands, and there he spent the next few minutes hitting balls off a tee. He then went to the Dodger dugout where he informed Lasorda that he was ready for pinch-hit duty.

That appeared unlikely as the first two Dodgers in the bottom of the ninth made outs, Scioscia popping out and Jeff Hamilton striking out. But pinch-hitter Mike Davis kept the Dodgers alive with a walk. And as 55,983 fans roared their approval, Gibson emerged from the dugout to pinch-hit.

Limping noticeably, Gibson hobbled to the plate where he would face Eckersley, owner of a league-leading 45 saves during the season and one of baseball's premier relievers of all time. Kirk not only could barely walk; he couldn't put weight on his legs when he swung the bat.

Gibson, however, was no stranger to tense situations. He had made a career of getting big hits. In his last World Series appearance in 1984 with the Tigers, he had blasted first- and eighth-inning home runs into the upper deck at Tiger Stadium in the fifth and deciding game with the San Diego Padres, driving in five runs altogether. He put the finishing touches on a spectacular game when he sprinted home from third with the go-ahead run after Alan Wiggins caught a fly in shallow right field in the fifth inning. Gibson's heroics sparked Detroit to an 8–4 victory and the club's first World Series triumph since 1967.

Eckersley's first three pitches were fastballs, and Gibson fouled each one off, falling behind in the count 0–2. Not only were Gibson's swings weak, but with each one, he staggered on his follow-through.

A ball outside, a foul, and two more balls sent the count to 3–2 as Davis stole second base. With first base open, Oakland manager Tony LaRussa could have walked Gibson at that point, but he chose not to do it. It was a critical mistake.

Eckersley threw a backdoor slider. Somehow Gibson turned on it, and with an awkward swing, sent a high drive to deep right. As Kirk watched, the ball cleared the right-field fence for a game-winning two-run homer.

"I didn't believe what I just saw," Eckersley said later. "It was just a terrible pitch."

Gibson staggered out of the box, stumbled as he rounded first, then seemed to pick up steam, yanking his arms in joyful celebration as he passed second. His legs hurt like crazy, but it didn't matter. Kirk chugged around third and finally careened across the plate into the waiting arms of his jubilant teammates.

"It was a great moment, the greatest of my career," Gibson said. "I feel fortunate to have been in there, and to be part of this."

The Dodgers had won, 5–4. More importantly, the home run turned the momentum squarely in L.A.'s favor. Lasorda's club went on to win three of the next four games as the big bats of Canseco and McGwire were held to a total of two hits. With Orel Hershiser collecting two of the verdicts, including a 5–2 decision in the clincher, the Dodgers had their second World Series triumph of the decade.

Gibson didn't play in the rest of the Series. But with one swing of the bat, he had made one of the most inspirational statements any hitter ever recorded.

In hitting a game-winning home run when he could barely stand, then triumphantly rounding the bases, Gibson had given baseball one of its most unforgettable moments. It was a sight no one who saw it will ever forget.

Oakland	AB	R	H	RBI
Lansford, 3b	4	1	0	0
Henderson, cf	5	0	2	0
Canseco, rf	4	1	1	4
Parker, lf	2	0	0	0
Javier, lf	1	0	1	0
McGwire, 1b	3	0	0	0
Steinbach, c	4	0	1	0
Hassey, c	0	0	0	0
Hubbard, 2b	4	1	2	0
Weiss, ss	4	0	0	0
Stewart, p	3	1	0	0
Eckersley, p	0	0	0	0
Totals	34	4	7	4

Los Angeles	AB	R	H	RBI
Sax, 2b	3	1	1	0
Stubbs, 1b	4	0	0	0
Hatcher, lf	3	1	1	2
Marshall, rf	4	1	1	0
Shelby, cf	4	0	1	0
Scioscia, c	4	0	1	1
Hamilton, 3b	4	0	0	0
Griffin, ss	2	0	1	0
Davis, ph	0	1	0	0
Belcher, p	0	0	0	0
Heep, ph	1	0	0	0
Leary, p	0	0	0	0
Woodson, ph	1	0	0	0
Holton, p	0	0	0	0
Gonzalez, ph	1	0	0	0
Pena, p	0	0	0	0
Gibson, ph	1	1	1	2
Totals	32	5	7	5

Oakland 0 4 0 0 0 0 0 0 0 **4**
Los Angeles 2 0 0 0 0 1 0 0 2 **5**
Two outs when winning run scored

Oakland	IP	H	R	ER	BB	SO
Stewart	8	6	3	3	2	5
Eckersley (L)	⅔*	1	2	2	1	1

Los Angeles	IP	H	R	ER	BB	SO
Belcher	2	3	4	4	4	3
Leary	3	3	0	0	1	3
Holton	2	0	0	0	1	0
Pena (W)	2	1	0	0	0	3

*Pitched to four batters in ninth

E–None. DP–Oakland 1. LOB–Oakland 10, Los Angeles 5. 2B–Henderson. HR–Canseco, Hatcher, Gibson. SB–Canseco, Sax, Davis. HBP–By Belcher (Canseco), By Stewart (Sax). B–Stewart. WP–Stewart. T–3:04. A–55,983.

Rick Dempsey

Marathon Ends in 22nd Inning

August 23, 1989 Olympic Stadium

Since the start of the 20th century, only 16 major league games have gone 22 innings or more. Only two reached the 22nd inning without any runs.

One of them was decided by a home run. It was delivered by Rick Dempsey in what is perhaps the most memorable homer ever hit in a game of that length.

Dempsey's blast gave the Los Angeles Dodgers a 1–0 victory over the Montreal Expos in a marathon affair August 23, 1989, at Olympic Stadium. Only eight major league games have ever been longer.

It was a game that had droned on hour after hour before finally ending six hours and 14 minutes after it had started. In terms of time, that made it the longest 1–0 game in baseball history.

Low-scoring games that extend at least 22 innings have been extremely rare. The longest game in baseball history was a 26-inning affair in 1920 that ended in a 1–1 tie between the Boston Braves and Brooklyn Dodgers. But only two other games of 22 or more innings have occurred in which each team scored one or fewer runs.

Prior to Dempsey's victorious swat, the longest shutout game in the majors had been an April 25, 1968, contest between the Houston Astros and New York Mets. Eventually, the Astros won, 1–0, in 24 innings. The game had lasted four hours and six minutes.

Ironically, the Dodgers—on their way to a fourth-place finish in the NL West—had already played in one 22-inning game in 1989. On June 3 they had bowed to the Astros, 5–4.

Dempsey was a most unlikely hero. At the time, he carried a batting average of .168. He wasn't even in the game at the start; in fact, didn't make an appearance until the eighth inning.

An accomplished catcher, Dempsey was closing in on the end of a long playing career during which he had spent all or parts of 24 seasons in the majors. A native of Tennessee, he had begun his professional career in 1967. In his early years, he put in several brief stints with the Minnesota Twins before landing as a backup catcher with the New York Yankees.

Dempsey was aquired in mid-1976 by the Baltimore Orioles as part of a 10-player trade with the Yanks. He spent the best years of his career with the Orioles, serving as the team's regular catcher through 1986. He then played with the Cleveland Indians, Dodgers, Milwaukee Brewers, and Orioles again before retiring as a player after the 1992 season with a .233 career batting average.

While he was with the Orioles, Dempsey had hit another memorable home run. His roundtripper in the fifth and final game of the 1983 World Series had helped Baltimore to a 5–0 win and the Series championship. Rick's .385 batting average had earned for him the Series Most Valuable Player award.

One of three catchers to play in four decades (the others are Tim McCarver and Carlton Fisk), Dempsey, who after retiring as a player was a minor league manager and scout before becoming a coach with the Dodgers in 1999, was not particularly noted as a home run hitter. His highest single-season total was 13, and he hit just 96 homers during his entire big league career.

But in the wee hours of the morning one summer night in Montreal, he was the toast of the fraternity of long-distance clouters.

The game, which began with a crowd of 21,742 in attendance, was one that frequently appeared on the brink of being over. But neither team could push across the deciding run.

"It was a very, very exciting game," Dodgers manager Tom Lasorda remembered. "Both teams had opportunities to score and couldn't do it.

So we just went on inning after inning with neither team scoring. It was just an amazing game."

Three times during the first 10 innings, the Dodgers had a runner get as far as third base only to be stranded. Montreal did it twice. In the 16th, the Expos appeared to have won the game when they loaded the bases with one out. Mike Fitzgerald then hit a fly ball to right fielder Mickey Hatcher. The throw to the plate was late, and rookie Larry Walker slid around Dempsey's tag. But Walker was called out by umpire Bob Davidson on an appeal play after the Dodgers claimed he had left third base too soon.

Hatcher reached third with two outs in the 19th, but could get no farther. Then in the 21st inning, Dodgers left fielder Lenny Harris made a fine running catch of a long drive by Andres Galarraga with a man on second and one out. One batter later, Dempsey threw out Tim Raines, who had walked, trying to steal second.

As the game progressed, a steady parade of pitchers marched to the mound for both teams. Orel Hershiser had started for the Dodgers, leaving after seven innings. Four more hurlers followed him to the mound before the game was over. Pascual Perez worked the first eight innings for the Expos ahead of five other pitchers.

"They went through just about every relief pitcher they had," said Dempsey. "It was kind of ironic that the guy who was doing the most yelling from their dugout was Dennis Martinez, one of their starters. He ended up in the game, I guess because it was his second day to throw."

Dempsey got into the game in the bottom of the eighth after starting catcher Mike Sciosia had been lifted for a pinch-runner. He singled to right and eventually reached third before being stranded in his first at-bat in the 10th. Rick struck out in his next two at-bats, then flew out to left and dropped a sacrifice bunt.

"The first eight innings of the game, I was sitting on the bench," said Dempsey. "Then I finally got in, and I ended up catching the last 14 innings."

The deciding blow came as Dempsey led off the top of the 22nd inning against Martinez, working in his second inning of relief. "He threw me a fastball, then a breaking ball," Dempsey recalled. "The count was 1–1. I figured he would come in with another fastball, and he did. That was the pitch I hit out of the park.

"I knew it was gone as soon as I hit it. The ball landed in the left-

One of baseball's longest games ended with a home run by **Rick Dempsey.**

center field stands, way back in the second section. That's a pretty good shot in Montreal. It was certainly one of the farthest balls I ever hit."

The shot was the 20th hit of the game for the Dodgers, but only their second extra-base hit. Coupled with the Expos' 13 hits, the marathon ended with 33 hits, only three for extra bases. Thirty-nine players appeared in the game.

"As soon as he hit it, you knew it was gone," said Lasorda. "He really hit that ball. There was no doubt about it."

The game, of course, wasn't over yet. And as Dempsey rounded the bases, he had only one thing on his mind. "I was just hoping it [the run] would hold up so we could get the heck out of there," he said. "It was already about 1:30 in the morning. We still had to take a plane back to Los Angeles."

After Dempsey's homer, the Dodgers went down in order. It wasn't over yet, though. John Wetteland, who was pitching in his sixth inning, retired the first two Expos batters in the bottom of the 22nd. But then he gave up a single to Rex Hudler. A moment later, Dempsey gunned down Hudler trying to steal second to end the game.

Interestingly, Wetteland, who later became one of his era's premier relievers, was then a starter, and had been scheduled to start the following night's game. Instead, he got the win in relief in a remarkable game.

In the end, there were 35 strikeouts in the game, 18 by the Expos. Dodger hurlers walked six. Montreal pitchers set a major league record for most innings pitched in a game without walking a batter. The previous mark was 21 innings set in 1914 by Babe Adams of the Pittsburgh Pirates.

Dempsey would hit only four home runs the entire season and finish with a .179 batting average. But that hardly seemed to matter.

"After the game, I showered and dressed, and then went out to get on the bus," Dempsey recalled. "Some of the players' wives were there, and they started hugging and kissing me because they were so happy we were finally going home.

"It had been a long night. We were all happy it was finally over."

Los Angeles	AB	R	H	RBI	Montreal	AB	R	H	RBI
Griffin, ss	9	0	0	0	Da. Martinez, cf	6	0	1	0
Randolph, 2b	9	0	2	0	Walker, rf	7	0	1	0
Harris, lf	9	0	5	0	Galarraga, 1b	9	0	1	0
Murray, 1b	9	0	3	0	Raines, lf	7	0	2	0
Hatcher, rf	9	0	1	0	Wallach, 3b	9	0	3	0
Scioscia, c	3	0	1	0	Fitzgerald, c	8	0	1	0
Bean, pr	0	0	0	0	Foley, 2b	5	0	1	0
Dempsey, c	5	1	2	1	Z. Smith, p	0	0	0	0
Hamilton, 3b	9	0	3	0	Grissom, ph	1	0	0	0
Gonzalez, cf	9	0	2	0	Thompson, p	0	0	0	0
Hershiser, p	2	0	0	0	Hudler, 2b	2	0	1	0
Sharperson, ph	1	0	0	0	Owen, ss	8	0	0	0
Howell, p	0	0	0	0	Perez, p	2	0	0	0
Anderson, ph	1	0	0	0	Johnson, ph	1	0	1	0
Pena, p	1	0	1	0	Nixon, pr	0	0	0	0
Huff, ph	1	0	0	0	Burke, p	0	0	0	0
Crews, p	0	0	0	0	Brooks, ph	1	0	0	0
Valenzuela, ph	1	0	0	0	B. Smith, p	0	0	0	0
Wetteland, p	2	0	0	0	Garcia, 2b	4	0	1	0
					De. Martinez, p	0	0	0	0
Totals	80	1	20	1		70	0	13	0

Los Angeles	0	0	0	0	0	0	0	0	0	0	0	0	0	0	0	0	0	0	0	0	0	1	**1**
Montreal	0	0	0	0	0	0	0	0	0	0	0	0	0	0	0	0	0	0	0	0	0	0	**0**

Los Angeles	IP	H	R	ER	BB	SO
Hershiser	7	4	0	0	2	6
Howell	2	2	0	0	0	0
Pena	4	2	0	0	0	5
Crews	3	3	0	0	2	3
Wetteland (W)	6	2	0	0	2	4
Montreal	**IP**	**H**	**R**	**ER**	**BB**	**SO**
Perez	8	7	0	0	0	7
Burke	2	3	0	0	0	1
B. Smith	2	4	0	0	0	2
Z. Smith	2	2	0	0	0	2
Thompson	6	3	0	0	0	3
De. Martinez (L)	2	1	1	1	0	2

E—Hershiser, Da. Martinez. DP—Los Angeles 4, Montreal 3. LOB—Los Angeles 14, Montreal 13. 2B—Hamilton, Wallach. HR—Dempsey. SB—Gonzalez. SF—Walker 2, Da. Martinez, Dempsey. T—6:14. A—21,742.

Joe Carter

Clutch Clout Gives Blue Jays the Series

October 23, 1993 SkyDome

Nothing in baseball occurs with quite the same finality as a game-winning home run in the bottom of the ninth inning. Coming suddenly and without warning, it delivers an absolute and unretractable conclusion. There is no more. The game is over. That's it.

Such an incontestable ending doesn't happen very often. It is a rare enough occurrence during the regular season, but it is virtually nonexistent in the World Series.

Only twice, since the first World Series was held in 1903, has a home run been hit on the final pitch of the last game. The most recent hitter to climb to such dramatic heights was Joe Carter. His three-run homer in the bottom of the ninth inning at the SkyDome gave the Toronto Blue Jays an 8–6 victory over the Philadelphia Phillies in the sixth and deciding game of the 1993 World Series.

Other home runs have won a World Series. But Carter's blast joined Bill Mazeroski's clout in 1960 as the only four-baggers to decide a fall classic in what turned out to be the final at-bat of the game.

"This is everything you dream about when you're playing the game," Carter said afterward. "It's something I'll remember the rest of my life."

For the Blue Jays, it was their second straight world championship, Toronto having beaten the Atlanta Braves in six games the year before. For the 33-year-old Carter, the homer climaxed a fine performance during which the hard-hitting right fielder had also homered in Game 2 and wound up the Series with eight RBI and a .280 batting average.

The homer, coming off Phillies reliever Mitch Williams, was not without controversy. Phils manager Jim Fregosi was roundly criticized for leaving the tiring and ineffective Williams in the game to face Carter, and for months afterward, he and the pitcher were showered with abuse from the highly critical Philadelphia fans. Williams even received threats on his life, and his house in New Jersey was stoned and egged by mindless crazies.

When it was hit, the home run didn't just overcome a 6–5 Phillies lead; it ended what had been one of the more bizarre World Series.

Toronto was at the end of the franchise's best era. The Blue Jays were the premier team in the American League and since 1985 had appeared in five League Championship Series. When the team won its second straight pennant in 1993 after beating the Chicago White Sox in a six-game LCS, it became the first club since the 1988–90 Oakland Athletics to win two or more AL flags in a row.

The Phillies hardly had matching credentials. Having struggled most of the time since their last pennant in 1983, they had finished in last place in the East Division in 1992, and were viewed as anything but a contender. But with a rollicking group of hard-nosed overachievers—gypsies, tramps, and thieves, they called themselves—the Phils had played at a .700 clip during the first three months of the season, easily won their division title, then defeated the mighty Braves four games to two to become only the third big league team in the 20th century to go from last to first in one year.

The Phillies and Blue Jays had numerous connections. Toronto had been a Phillies farm team more than 40 years earlier. The Phils had been briefly—although unofficially— called the Blue Jays back in the 1940s. For many years the two teams had trained in adjoining towns in Florida and were frequent opponents in the Grapefruit League. And Blue Jays third base coach Nick Leyva had been the Phillies manager until replaced in 1991 by Fregosi (who later became Toronto's manager).

The Blue Jays had a strong offensive team. En route to a 95–67 record during the regular season, they led the league with a .279 batting average with Paul Molitor and John Olerud each getting 200 or more hits and dri-

Joe Carter was only the second player to end a World Series in his team's last at-bat.

ving in more than 100 runs apiece. Carter also reached the 100-RBI level during the regular season, hitting .254 with 33 home runs.

The Phillies were no slouches on offense, either. John Kruk, Lenny Dykstra, Jim Eisenreich, and Kevin Stocker all hit over .300, while Darren Daulton, Pete Incaviglia, and Dave Hollins supplied much of the power.

Offense was very much in the picture as the Series began. In a game that featured 21 hits, the Blue Jays captured an 8–5 decision. The Phils came back with a 6–4 win in the second game, but Toronto returned to the winner's circle in Game 3 with a 10–3 romp. The Blue Jays then took a 3–1 lead in the Series in an extraordinary 15–14 slugfest that was the highest scoring and longest nine-inning game in World Series history. The Phillies appeared doomed, but Curt Schilling came up with a brilliant five-hit, complete game shutout to beat the Blue Jays, 2–0, and send the Series back to Toronto.

The conclusive Game 6 turned out to be in perfect step with the rest of the oddball Series. The Blue Jays with the help of a Carter sacrifice fly took a 3–0 lead in the first inning. After five innings, Toronto had a 5–1 advantage.

But in a wild seventh inning, the Phillies launched a comeback, sending 10 men to the plate and knocking out ace Toronto hurler Dave Stewart. The big blow was a three-run homer by Dykstra—his fourth of the Series. By the time the inning was over, the Phils had scored five runs and had clawed to a 6–5 lead.

By this time, Roger Mason had relieved Phils starter Terry Mulholland and was in the midst of a strong outing in which he would allow just one hit in 1⅔ innings of work. With no one on base and one out in the eighth, however, Fregosi lifted Mason, setting the stage for what would become an endless debate.

Phillies relievers David West and Larry Andersen proceeded to load the bases before escaping without damage. But the real damage had been done. The effective Mason was out of the game, and in the ninth Fregosi brought in Williams.

Williams had enjoyed a marvelous season, setting a club record with 43 saves. But a season of hard throwing had taken its toll, and the Phillies southpaw was virtually out of gas. He had been credited with a save in Game 2, but had been charged with the loss in Game 4 and was now throwing with nowhere near his normal speed.

Always pitching on the wild side anyway, Williams walked Rickey Henderson to start the ninth. Devon White flied out to left, but Molitor followed with a single. It was now Carter's turn. Joe had no hits in three previous trips to the plate.

Carter worked the count to 2–2, swinging badly on the second strike. On Williams' next offering, Carter pounded the ball into the left-field stands for a three-run homer. With one swing of the bat, Carter had not only erased a Phillies one-run lead, he had given Toronto a World Series victory.

"As soon as I hit it, I lost it," Carter said. "I thought I got all of it, but I wasn't sure. Then I picked it up, and saw it was high enough to clear the fence. I just started jumping up and down.

"With Mitch out there, you knew something good would happen," Carter added. "I knew his velocity was not good. The only pitch he was throwing for strikes was a slider. He threw me a 2–1 slider that I missed. Then I told myself, 'All I need is a base hit.' He threw me a slider down and in. I was kind of hunched down with the swing because I was staying down with the pitch. I was just hoping I hit it well enough."

"It was a weird feeling, watching that ball go out," said Dykstra. "Helpless. I can't really describe it. I didn't want to watch it."

Although it was a devastating loss for the Phillies and particularly Williams, the Phils lefthander neither alibied nor apologized for the pitch he threw. "There are no excuses," he said. "I just didn't get the job done. It was a bad pitch. I'll have to deal with it. The one thing that bothers me is I let my teammates down. I threw the pitch that cost us the World Series. But don't expect me to curl up and hide because I gave up a home run in the World Series. I can carry the burden. And going home and sulking about it does not bring the ball back over the fence."

At least publicly, Williams' teammates stood behind him. "We wouldn't have been here if it wasn't for him," Kruk said in the kind of statement Phillies players repeated over and over.

"He has nothing to hang his head about," added Daulton. "That guy [Carter] gets paid to hit, and he came out on top this time. You have to tip your hat to him."

But the debate over whether or not Fregosi should have left Mason in the game raged in Philadelphia all winter. Fregosi defended himself by saying Williams was his best, and he had to go with his best. Many agreed, many didn't.

As for Williams, the Phils would trade him during the off-season, and he would never again pitch with the same effectiveness with which he had. For the Blue Jays and Phillies, it was their last year in the limelight. Both teams slipped dramatically in the standings the following year, and for the rest of the decade they performed well below the levels of contention.

Carter continued as a forceful hitter until retiring after the 1998 season. During his 16-year career, he slugged home runs in double figures in 15 consecutive seasons, finishing with a career total of 396 during the regular season.

It was the one in postseason, however, that stood out above all the others.

Phillies	AB	R	H	RBI	Toronto	AB	R	H	RBI
Dykstra, cf	3	1	1	3	Henderson, lf	4	1	0	0
Duncan, dh	5	1	1	0	White, cf	4	1	0	0
Kruk, 1b	3	0	0	0	Molitor, dh	5	3	3	2
Hollins, 3b	5	1	1	1	Carter, rf	4	1	1	4
Batiste, 3b	0	0	0	0	Olerud, 1b	3	1	1	0
Daulton, c	4	1	1	0	Griffin, pr, 3b	0	0	0	0
Eisenreich, rf	5	0	2	1	Alomar, 2b	4	1	3	1
Thompson, lf	3	0	0	0	Fernandez, ss	3	0	0	0
Incaviglia, ph, lf	0	0	0	1	Sprague, 3b, 1b	2	0	0	1
Stocker, ss	3	1	0	0	Borders, c	4	0	2	0
Morandini, 2b	4	1	1	0	Stewart, p	0	0	0	0
Mulholland, p	0	0	0	0	Cox, p	0	0	0	0
Mason, p	0	0	0	0	Leiter, p	0	0	0	0
West, p	0	0	0	0	Ward, p	0	0	0	0
Andersen, p	0	0	0	0					
Williams, p	0	0	0	0					
Totals	35	6	7	6		33	8	10	8

Philadelphia	0 0 0 1 0 0 5 0 0 **6**
Toronto	3 0 0 1 1 0 0 0 3 **8**

Philadelphia	IP	H	R	ER	BB	SO
Mulholland	5	7	5	1	1	1
Mason	2⅓	1	0	0	0	2
West	0*	0	0	0	1	0
Andersen	⅔	0	0	0	1	0
Williams (L)	⅓	2	3	3	1	0
Toronto	**IP**	**H**	**R**	**ER**	**BB**	**SO**
Stewart	6†	4	4	4	4	2
Cox	⅓	3	2	2	1	1
Leiter	1⅔	0	0	0	1	2
Ward (W)	1	0	0	0	0	0

*Pitched to one batter in eighth
†Pitched to three batters in seventh

E–Alomar, Sprague. LOB–Philadelphia 9, Toronto 7. 2B–Daulton, Olerud, Alomar. 3B–Molitor. HR–Molitor, Carter, Dykstra. SB–Dykstra, Duncan. SF–Incaviglia, Carter, Sprague. HBP–By Andersen (Fernandez). T–3:26. A–52,195.

Cal Ripken

Homer Accompanies Record-Setting Streak

September 6, 1995 Camden Yards

Memorable home runs usually occur when the spotlight shines brightly. For Cal Ripken, the spotlight couldn't have been any brighter.

Ripken had been the center of attention long before he came upon that memorable September 6, 1995, night at Baltimore's Camden Yards. The Orioles shortstop had been the object of a nationwide watch for several years as he closed in on one of major league baseball's most hallowed records—the one that was generally considered least likely to be broken.

The record, of course, was Lou Gehrig's streak of 2,130 consecutive games played. The streak, accumulated between 1925 and 1939, did not have a serious challenger after it came to an abrupt conclusion when the great New York Yankees slugger was found to be suffering from ALS. In fact, no one had ever come remotely close to the mark until Ripken began making signs that he might break it.

Since May 30, 1982, the sturdy Orioles star had not missed a game. Year in and year out, month after month, day after day, he had played every game on the Baltimore schedule, fighting off injury, fatigue, criticism that he was hurting his team, and occasionally a manager's desire to bench him.

Along the way, he played in a record 8,243 consecutive innings. He played a record 95 straight games without an error. And with a truckload of awards and postseason honors, he set himself up for a certain spot in the Hall of Fame.

Ripken moved into second place on the all-time list of consecutive games played in 1990 when he appeared in his 1,308th straight contest. The streak continued to build thereafter, and by the start of the 1995 season, Gehrig's "Iron Man" record was in serious trouble. Ripken had played in his 2,000th game on August 1 the previous year, and if he stayed healthy, he figured to break the mark late in the '95 season.

As September began, that opportunity was finally about to arrive. The Orioles were far out of contention for a playoff spot in the American League East Division, so as a three-game series began against the California Angels, all the attention was focused on Ripken.

The pressure that now surrounded Ripken had built to an excruciatingly high level. Never one to show at least outwardly how tense the situation really was, Ripken was besieged by fans, the media, and legions of others making endless demands on his time and energy.

A quiet, introspective person, Ripken was able to fend off much of the commotion that surrounded him. He even warmed to the occasion by hitting a home run in each of the first two games of the series while equaling Gehrig's record in the second game on September 5. The stage was set for Ripken to break the 56-year-old record in the third game.

Tickets to the game were as scarce as a Sunday doubleheader. Among the sellout crowd of 46,272 who did get them, prominent figures were scattered throughout the stands. President Bill Clinton was there, along with Vice President Al Gore, perhaps marking the first time the nation's two highest officeholders were in attendance at the same sporting event. A huge array of baseball dignitaries, including Gehrig's old teammate Joe DiMaggio and some of Ripken's 1982 teammates, also attended.

"These are the kinds of people who make America great," Clinton said in reference to Ripken, who hit home runs in double figures in every one of his 18 big league seasons through 1999.

Righthander Shawn Boskie was on the mound for the Angels, facing the Orioles' Mike Mussina before a nationwide television audience. Ripken, who was showered with gifts before the game, carried a .268 batting average with 14 home runs into the contest.

In his first trip to the plate in the second inning, the 38-year-old Rip-

Cal Ripken homered in the same game in which he broke Lou Gehrig's streak.

ken, playing in his 14th big league season, popped out. With the fans cheering loudly before and after each at-bat, he came to the plate again in the fourth, with the game—and hence his streak—not yet official.

Bobby Bonilla had led off the inning with a home run to give the Orioles a 2–1 lead. Ripken was the next batter, and Boskie threw three straight balls. Then on a 3–0 count he grooved a fastball in the middle of the strike zone, and Ripken drilled a shot that reached the stands in deep left.

For Ripken, who on the wings of the streak had risen to the status of a national hero, it was his third homer in three games, a feat he had last accomplished in 1991. The blast ultimately gave Baltimore the winning margin in a 4–2 victory in a game in which Rafael Palmeiro hit two solo homers for the Orioles.

"You derive the most satisfaction from winning and being part of a winning team," Ripken said. "Winning is what it's all about. Having the opportunity to shake hands on the field after a victory is what makes it all worthwhile. Throw that in with the rest of the celebration, and everything came out nice."

Few homers in the history of baseball have ever been hit under more intense pressure and in such dramatic circumstances. Nor have there been many times when a home run came in a more emotional setting.

"There's no doubt about it," Ripken said later in answer to a question about the importance of the dramatic home run. "It made the celebration, it made the event, it made everything so much better."

The home run provided Ripken with a perfect way to punctuate his extraordinary night. But the festivities hardly stopped there. Twelve minutes later, the game reached the bottom of the fifth inning to become official, allowing Ripken's new record to go into the books. As it did, play was stopped, fireworks were launched, and a 22-minute celebration began. It ended with Ripken taking a victory lap around the interior of the stadium as players from both teams clapped and fans gave him a standing ovation.

Soon after the game resumed, Ripken popped out with the bases loaded to end the inning. Cal then came to bat once more in the game, hitting a single in the eighth inning.

Following the final out, an hour-long celebration was held. Speeches were made, and more gifts were presented as Ripken and his family and a long list of special guests congregated near home plate.

"Wherever he [Gehrig] is, I'm sure he tipped his cap to you," an uncharacteristically tearful DiMaggio told Ripken.

In his own speech, Ripken, before riding one last lap around the stadium in an open convertible, also referred to the man whose legendary streak he had just broken. "I stand here overwhelmed as my name is linked with the great and courageous Lou Gehrig," Ripken said. "I'm truly humbled to have our names mentioned in the same breath.

"I know that if Lou Gehrig is looking down on tonight's activities, he isn't concerned about someone playing one more consecutive game than he did. Instead, he's viewing tonight as just another example of what is good and right about the great American game. Whether your name is Gehrig or Ripken, DiMaggio or Robinson, or that of some youngster who picks up his bat or puts on his glove, you are challenged by the game of baseball to do your very best day in and day out. And that's all I've ever tried to do."

Ripken's very best also had special significance in another way. The previous season, baseball had suffered a withering strike, which had extended into the 1995 season. Disgruntled fans stayed away in droves from the nation's big league ballparks, and public interest in the game was severely damaged.

Ripken played a major role in helping to save baseball from disaster and to rekindle the fans' enthusiasm for the game. As the record approached and the focus of the streak intensified, many baseball fans were attracted back to the game, watching avidly as a new national hero took center stage.

With his work ethic, his apparently immense inner strength, his clean-cut image, and his superb playing skills, Ripken was the perfect choice to lead the tarnished game of baseball back into a position of favor in the hearts of sports fans. And that's precisely what he did.

The streak itself continued until close to the end of the 1998 season. Although by then he had switched to third base, Ripken removed himself from the lineup on September 20 after playing in 2,632 consecutive games. During the streak, Ripken had left games early only 66 times.

A two-time Most Valuable Player award winner and a 16-time member of the American League All-Star team, Ripken ended the 1998 season with more home runs (345) than any other shortstop in baseball history. At the end of the 1999 season he had a career total of 402.

None, however, attracted any greater attention nor came under any brighter spotlight than the one he hit on that pressure-packed night when he broke one of baseball's most enduring records.

California	AB	R	H	RBI
Phillips, 3b	4	0	0	0
Edmonds, cf	3	1	1	0
Salmon, rf	4	1	3	2
Davis, dh	3	0	0	0
Snow, 1b	4	0	1	0
G. Anderson, lf	4	0	0	0
Hudler, 2b	2	0	0	0
Owens, ph, 2b	2	0	0	0
Fabregas, c	3	0	0	0
Easley, ss	2	0	1	0
O. Palmeiro, ph	1	0	0	0
Correia, ss	0	0	0	0
Boskie, p	0	0	0	0
Bielecki, p	0	0	0	0
Patterson, p	0	0	0	0
James, p	0	0	0	0
Totals	32	2	6	2

Baltimore	AB	R	H	RBI
B. Anderson, cf	4	0	1	0
Alexander, 2b	4	0	0	0
R. Palmeiro, 1b	4	2	3	2
Bonilla, rf	4	1	1	1
Brown, rf	0	0	0	0
Ripken, ss	4	1	2	1
Baines, dh	4	0	1	0
Hoiles, c	4	0	1	0
Huson, 3b	4	0	0	0
Smith, lf	2	0	0	0
Mussina, p	0	0	0	0
Clark, p	0	0	0	0
Orosco, p	0	0	0	0
Totals	34	4	9	4

California 1 0 0 0 0 0 0 1 0 **2**
Baltimore 1 0 0 2 0 0 1 0 x **4**

California	IP	H	R	ER	BB	SO
Boskie (L)	5	6	3	3	1	4
Bielecki	1	1	0	0	0	2
Patterson	⅔	1	1	1	0	1
James	1⅓	1	0	0	0	1

Baltimore	IP	H	R	ER	BB	SO
Mussina (W)	7⅔	5	2	2	2	7
Clark	0*	1	0	0	0	0
Orosco	1⅓	0	0	0	0	2

*Pitched to one batter in eighth

E–Phillips. DP–Baltimore 1. LOB–California 5, Baltimore 7. 2B–Salmon, Easley, Baines. 3B–Edmonds. HR–R. Palmeiro 2. Ripken, Salmon. T–3:35. A–46,272.

Mark McGwire

An Incredible 70–Home Run Season

September 27, 1998 Busch Stadium

In the long history of the sport of baseball, it is doubtful that any home run attracted more attention—both nationally and around the world—than the one Mark McGwire drilled in his final at-bat of the 1998 season.

It is equally unlikely that any home run was ever more dramatic or carried with it such a weighted impact. When McGwire cracked a line drive over the left-field fence in the seventh inning of the final game of the season at St. Louis's Busch Stadium on September 27, 1998, an achievement of the most improbable proportions had taken place.

The homer on that storied day was the 70th of the season for the muscular St. Louis Cardinals first baseman. It elevated him to a level so far beyond anyone else that it was almost too amazing to comprehend.

Seventy home runs in one season? The conventional wisdom has always considered that level impossible to reach. No one in the major leagues ever even approached it before. In fact, even hitting 60 home runs in one season is a feat only two people had accomplished prior to the 1998 season.

But, if there was ever an ideal candidate to make a run at 70, Big Mac was it. A huge man standing 6–5 and weighing 250 pounds, he has the strength of a Paul Bunyan and wrists as quick as lightning. With a mere flick of his powerful arms, he can send majestic, towering drives to the most remote parts of any ballpark on the planet. It helps that in addition to his amazing power, he has virtually no wasted movement in his swing, and he has the gift of being able to see the ball especially well.

Although he had suffered several major injuries in the 1990s, McGwire can be devastating when healthy. In 1987 his league-leading 49 home runs with the Oakland Athletics were the most any rookie ever hit. He led the American League with 52 home runs while still at Oakland in 1996. And in 1997, while splitting the season between the A's and Cardinals, he connected for a combined total of 58 round-trippers, becoming the first player since 1961 to hit that many home runs in a single campaign.

The strapping righthander from California, who hit a home run in his very first at-bat in baseball as a 10-year-old Little Leaguer and who was originally a pitcher, kept up the pace as the 1998 season got under way. He hit a game-winning grand slam on opening day. By the end of May, after three–home run games against Arizona and Philadelphia, he already had 27 dingers. By the beginning of September, his total was up to 55, and McGwire had become the first player in baseball history ever to clout 50 or more homers in three consecutive seasons. Setting a new home run record seemed a virtual certainty.

All the while, McGwire was waging a torrid duel for the home run leadership with Chicago Cubs right fielder Sammy Sosa. For much of the season, the two stayed close with seldom more than a few home runs separating their totals. They also grew into good friends, interacting in a way few other opponents ever did and celebrating each other's accomplishments with a true spirit of sportsmanship.

When the season had started, baseball in general had still not fully recovered from the distasteful effects of the 1994 work stoppage. Many fans were still shunning the sport, but the riveting home run race helped to restore interest in the game and bring it back to prestrike levels.

"It was like playing in a World Series every day for three months," said left fielder Ron Gant, who in 1998 batted behind McGwire in the lineup. "But Mark never let it get to him. He withstood the pressure and handled everything very gracefully. He's a strong person, mentally as well as physically."

With the Cardinals playing poorly, McGwire was free to swing for the fences. The only real distraction during the season was the revelation that he took legal muscle-enchancing drugs, which are permitted by major league baseball although not in some other sports.

McGwire's mightly clouts continued to pepper distant bleachers as the season progessed. He hit his 60th home run off Dennis Reyes in a 7–0 win over the Cincinnati Reds on September 5 at Busch Stadium. Two days later, as Sosa stood and applauded, he equaled Roger Maris's record of 61 with a blast off Mike Morgan in a 3–2 victory over the Chicago Cubs, also at Busch Stadium. McGwire had reached his number 61 in his 144th game (19 fewer than it took Maris).

Maris's record was broken on September 8 when McGwire connected for his 62nd homer off the Cubs' Steve Trachsel as the Cards won, 6–3. McGwire hit a low liner that just cleared the fence in left field. As he circled the bases, almost missing first as he ran, Cubs infielders shook his hand. Arriving at home plate, McGwire hoisted his young son Matthew, serving as a Cardinals batboy, in the air. Sosa arrived from right field, and the two embraced near home plate. Then, after pointing to the sky in an emotional tribute to the deceased Maris, McGwire ran to the box where the ex–New York Yankee slugger's four sons and two daughters stood applauding.

In an era of crass commercialism and sickeningly unprofessional hype, McGwire's high regard for the sanctity of the record and his gracious acceptance of the crown he now wore couldn't have been more admirable. But the new home run king was far from done. Sosa tied him briefly at 62 as the two home run sluggers battled down the stretch. Then Sosa moved ahead once more, only to fall behind. On the last Friday of the season, Sosa took a 66–65 lead, but less than one hour later, McGwire had pulled to a tie.

On the next-to-last day of the season at St. Louis, McGwire socked two homers, one off Dustin Hermanson, the other off Kirk Bullinger, as the Cards dropped a 7–6 decision to the Montreal Expos. Mark's total stood at 68 as the Cardinals again faced the Expos on the final day of the season.

Seemingly the whole world was watching. With television cameras whirling and the 14th straight sellout crowd packing Busch Stadium, McGwire added his 69th home run on a towering drive into the left-field stands off rookie Mike Thurman in the third inning.

The best, though, was still to come. With two outs, two men on, and the score tied in the seventh inning, McGwire stepped to the plate against

Mark McGwire became the first player ever to hit 70 home runs in one season.

Carl Pavano, a highly regarded rookie righthander the Expos had acquired during the off-season in a trade with the Boston Red Sox for ace pitcher Pedro Martinez.

Pavano's first pitch was a 96-mile-per-hour fastball. The ball was traveling even faster after Big Mac hit it. McGwire launched a screaming drive into the left-field stands and suddenly—astonishingly—a feat that had not been thought to be possible had occurred.

McGwire danced joyfully around the bases, Expos infielders congratulating him as he passed. Finally arriving at home with the run that gave the Cardinals a 6–3 victory, McGwire was treated to a standing ovation that lasted for five minutes. There was pandemonium in the stands, and in virtually every other corner of the globe where the game was being watched.

"I can't believe I did it," an incredulous McGwire told a massive gathering of reporters after the game. "It's absolutely amazing. It just blows me away.

"Hitting 70," McGwire added, "is something I never even thought about. I never even dreamed about it."

Pavano, who had served McGwire his 66th home run a few days earlier after not having allowed a circuit clout in the previous month, had trouble believing what had happened, too. "I was going to go right after him," he said. "As it turned out, he went right after me."

For McGwire, the home run was the fifth in his last 11 at-bats. He had ended the season with the most stunning of flourishes, hitting 15 homers during September while performing under enormously pressurized conditions.

During the season, the usually reserved McGwire had 10 multi–home run games. He finished the year with a .299 batting average, 147 RBI and 130 runs scored. Significantly, McGwire drew 162 walks during the season (while striking out 155 times). And his .752 slugging percentage was the highest of any big league player since Ruth and Lou Gehrig's 1927 totals.

With the Cardinals finishing a weak third in the National League's Central Division, McGwire was edged out in the Most Valuable Player voting by Sosa, whose Cubs managed to gain a spot in the postseason playoffs. But Sosa's honor hardly diminished the impact of McGwire's unbelievable season.

"It's amazing," said McGwire, "that a guy who just swings the bat could have this impact on the country and on people's lives."

But he did. In an incredible season climaxed by a most remarkable ending, McGwire had the kind of impact that was perhaps unprecedented in all of sports.

Montreal	AB	R	H	RBI	St. Louis	AB	R	H	RBI
W. Guerrero, 2b	5	1	2	0	McEwing, 2b, lf	3	2	2	0
Jones, cf	5	0	1	0	Drew, rf, cf	4	1	2	0
May, lf	3	1	0	0	McGwire, 1b	3	2	3	4
Perez, lf	1	0	0	0	Kelly, 2b	0	0	0	0
V. Guerrero, rf	4	0	2	1	Jordan, cf	4	0	0	1
Sequignoi, rf	0	0	0	0	Little, rf	0	0	0	0
Fulmer, 1b	4	0	1	0	Gant, lf	3	0	1	0
Barrett, c	3	0	1	1	King, p	0	0	0	0
Andrews, 3b	3	0	1	0	McGee, ph	0	0	0	0
Cabrera, ss	4	1	1	1	Lankford, ph	1	0	0	0
Thurman, p	2	0	0	0	Acevedo, p	0	0	0	0
Vidro, ph	1	0	0	0	Tatis, 3b	4	1	1	1
Pavano, p	0	0	0	0	Ordaz, ss	4	0	0	0
McGuire, ph	1	0	0	0	Morris, p	1	0	0	0
Telford, p	0	0	0	0	DeShields, ph	1	0	0	0
					Frascatore, p	0	0	0	0
					Mabry, ph, lf, 1b	2	0	0	0
					Marrero, c	3	0	0	0
					Lampkin, c	0	0	0	0
Totals	36	3	9	3		33	6	9	6

	1	2	3	4	5	6	7	8	9	R
Montreal	0	0	2	1	0	0	0	0	0	**3**
St. Louis	1	1	1	0	0	0	3	0	x	**6**

Montreal	IP	H	R	ER	BB	SO
Thurman	5	6	3	3	1	3
Pavano (L)	2	3	3	3	0	2
Telford	1	0	0	0	0	1

St. Louis	IP	H	R	ER	BB	SO
Morris	4	6	3	3	3	2
Frascatore (W)	3	3	0	0	0	2
King	1	0	0	0	0	1
Acevedo	1	0	0	0	0	0

E–Andrews, Tatis, Ordaz. DP–St. Louis 1. LOB–Montreal 9, St. Louis 5. 2B–Barrett, Drew, Gant. HR–Cabrera, McGwire 2, Tatis. SB–Jordan. HBP–By Thurman (McEwing). WP–Morris. T–2:33. A–46,110.

Fernando Tatis

Two Grand Slams in the Same Inning

April 23, 1999 Dodger Stadium

Of all the batters who have etched their names into a special place in home run history, none was more improbable or more unknown than third baseman Fernando Tatis of the St. Louis Cardinals.

Prior to the 1999 season, few outside of St. Louis knew much about the 24-year-old native of the Dominican Republic. He was hardly a familiar name on a Cardinals team that had its share of notables.

Tatis certainly wasn't known for his long-distance clouting. In 755 big league at-bats prior to 1999, he had just 19 home runs. He had never hit a grand slam. And he had only 61 dingers during just under five seasons in the minors.

But on April 23, 1999, at Dodger Stadium, Tatis performed a feat never previously done in the history of major league baseball. The 5–10, 170-pounder slugged two grand-slam home runs in one inning.

Leading up to that spectacular performance, there had been 4,777 grand-slam homers hit since major league play began. No player ever hit two in the same inning. In fact, only nine players had ever hit two in the same game.

"You have a better chance of winning the lottery," said another home

Fernando Tatis performed a feat never previously done in major league baseball.

run hitter of distinction, Mark McGwire, who batted ahead of Tatis in the Cardinals' lineup.

In the 20th century, two grand slams have been hit in the same inning only four times (in 1962 by the Minnesota Twins, in 1969 by the Houston Astros, in 1980 by the Milwaukee Brewers, and in 1986 by the Baltimore Orioles). But those were hit by different players.

Although 20 other National Leaguers have done it, no St. Louis Cardinal ever hit two home runs of any kind in one inning. And only once—in 1929 when Jim Bottomley and Chick Hafey did it—have the Redbirds registered two grand slams in the same game.

Tatis's extraordinary achievement not only earned a prominent place as one of baseball's most memorable home run displays, but it also carved a niche in the RBI section of the record book. By driving in eight runs in one inning, Tatis shattered the modern record of six RBI in one inning, a mark previously held by 13 different players.

"What an accomplishment," said Cardinals manager Tony LaRussa. "I get goose pimples just thinking about it."

Los Angeles Dodgers pitcher Chan Ho Park, who entered the game with a 1–1 record, served both of Tatis's homers, a dubious distinction no other 20th-century pitcher can claim. The Pittsburgh Pirates' Bill Phillips, pitching against the Chicago Cubs, is the only other major league hurler ever to surrender two slams in the same inning, and that was more than 100 years ago in 1890.

The righthanded-hitting Tatis, who was batting .264 entering the game, was hitting out of the cleanup spot in the St. Louis order. But even that was a bit unexpected. The Cards' regular cleanup hitter, Eric Davis, had a sore hand and couldn't play, allowing Tatis to be moved up one notch in the lineup.

A native of the baseball-rich city of San Pedro de Marcorís, Tatis was only in his second full season in the majors. Originally signed by the Texas Rangers, he was twice named that club's minor league player of the year before making the jump from Double-A to the big leagues midway through the 1997 season.

A little more than one year later, the Rangers traded Tatis to the Cardinals in a five-player deal that also brought Royce Clayton and Todd Stottlemyre to St. Louis. Tatis finished the season with an overall batting average of .276 with 11 home runs.

Tatis, whose father Fernando was also a professional player who got as far as the high minors in the Houston Astros system, had four home runs in the first 14 games of the 1999 season. Then came that remarkable game in L.A.

The Cardinals were scoreless in their first two at-bats, but in the third with Tatis leading the charge, they exploded with 11 runs (six short of the modern major league record). Six of the runs were unearned.

Darren Bragg began the inning with a single. Edgar Renteria was hit by a pitch, and McGwire followed with a check-swing single to right to load the bases. That brought up Tatis, and he responded by launching a 2–0 fastball well over the left-field wall. Had it not hit the back wall of the bullpen, the 450-foot drive would have left the park altogether.

Tatis wasn't the only St. Louis homer hitter. One out after the slam, Eli Marrero clubbed another Park pitch over the left-field wall. Park then walked the next two batters before eventual winning pitcher Jose Jimenez dropped an intended sacrifice bunt. The Dodgers hurler fielded the ball, but threw it wide of third, and the bases were again loaded.

Dodger first baseman Eric Karros then scooped up Bragg's grounder, but when his throw home pulled catcher Todd Hundley off the plate, another run scored and another error was charged. Dodgers manager Dave Johnson was ejected from the game for arguing the call at the plate.

Renteria followed with a single. One run came home on the hit, but Jimenez was held up at third, although he had plenty of time to score, too.

That was a break for Tatis because it kept the bases loaded. When home run king McGwire lofted an easy fly to shallow right and Jimenez was again held, Tatis had yet another stroke of good fortune.

Park was still on the mound as Tatis batted for the second time in the inning. This time, Tatis worked a 3–2 count before unloading a 375-foot shot into the left-center-field bleachers.

The blow kayoed Park, who had faced 13 batters in the inning. "It was just a terrible day," the beleaguered pitcher said later in a splendid case of understatement.

St. Louis would score only once more the rest of the game, on a home run by J. D. Drew, while cruising to a 12–5 victory. It was a victory that belonged to Tatis. "I can't believe it happened," he said. "After the first one, I didn't expect to hit another. I was just trying to meet the ball."

Recalling how LaRussa had told him before the game "to be patient" at the plate, Tatis said that he was trying to hit a home run the first time, and had no doubt the ball would clear the wall after he hit it.

"I was looking for a fastball inside, and he threw it there, and I hit it. On the second one, he threw a slider inside, and I wasn't expecting it. I just tried to line it. I didn't think I had enough explosion, so I didn't think it was going out. I started running, and then I realized it was out."

And Tatis had hit himself into the record book with a feat never before accomplished in the more than 120 years of major league baseball. "Any ballplayer is looking to be famous," he said. "You want your name to get bigger and bigger. I think my name is going to be famous."

Tatis homered again in the next game, and would briefly even pass McGwire as the Cardinals home run leader. Later in the season, he added another grand slam.

The young St. Louis slugger finished the season with a .298 batting average and 34 home runs, which broke by two the Cardinals all-time record for a third baseman. None of the other homers, however, quite attracted the notoriety of the two grand slams in one inning.

St. Louis	AB	R	H	RBI	Los Angeles	AB	R	H	RBI
Bragg, rf	5	2	3	0	Young, 2b	4	1	2	1
Renteria, ss	5	2	1	1	Cromer, rf	1	0	0	0
McGwire, 1b	5	1	1	0	Vizcaino, ss, 2b	3	0	2	0
Aybar, p	0	0	0	0	Sheffield, lf	2	0	0	1
Tatis, 3b	5	2	2	8	Hollingsworth, ph, lf	2	0	0	1
Drew, cf	4	1	2	1	Mondesi, rf	4	0	0	0
Marrero, c, 1b	5	1	2	1	Kubenka, p	0	0	0	0
Howard, 2b	0	0	0	0	LoDuca, ph	1	0	0	0
Polanco, ph, 2b	3	1	0	0	Karros, 1b	3	0	1	0
McEwing, lf	4	1	0	0	Hansen, 1b	1	1	1	0
Jimenez, p	3	1	0	0	White, cf	3	1	2	0
Castillo, c	1	0	0	0	Brumfield, cf	1	0	0	0
					Beltre, 3b	4	1	2	1
					Hundley, c	3	0	0	1
					Park, p	1	0	0	0
					Perez, p	1	0	0	0
					Grudzielanek, ph, ss	1	1	1	0
Totals	40	12	11	11		35	5	11	5

St. Louis	0	0	11	0	0	1	0	0	0	**12**
Los Angeles	1	1	0	0	0	0	2	1	0	**5**

St. Louis	IP	H	R	ER	BB	SO
Jimenez (W)	7	9	4	3	1	6
Aybar	2	2	1	1	0	2
Los Angeles	**IP**	**H**	**R**	**ER**	**BB**	**SO**
Park (L)	2⅔	8	11	6	3	2
Perez	4⅓	3	1	1	0	4
Kubenka	2	0	0	0	2	1

E–Bragg, Vizcaino 2, Karros. LOB–St. Louis 8, Los Angeles 8. 2B–Bragg, Drew, Hansen. HR–Drew, Marrero, Tatis 2. SB–Marrero, McEwing. SF–Jimenez, Vizcaino. SFF–Sheffield, Hundley. HBP–By Aybar (Grudzielanek), By Park (Renteria). T–3:05. A–46,687.

Sammy Sosa

First Player to Reach 60 Home Runs Twice

September 18, 1999, Wrigley Field

It is an extremely remarkable feat when a player hits 60 or more home runs in one season. After all, before 1998, only two people had ever done it.

But when the same player performs the feat two years in a row, the achievement becomes downright extraordinary. It stretches into the realm of fantasy. It borders on the unbelievable.

In 1999, in the second great home run race of the 1990s, Sammy Sosa did what no other hitter had ever done before when he blasted his 60th homer for the second straight year. No other hitter had ever hit 60 homers twice in a career, much less 60 in back-to-back seasons.

Sosa, who in 1998 capped a spectacular season by hitting 66 home runs, while finishing second to Mark McGwire, socked his second 60th off Jason Bere of the Milwaukee Brewers on September 18, 1999, at Wrigley Field in a 7–4 Chicago Cubs loss in 14 innings. The sixth-inning solo blast came after Sosa had gone hitless in his previous 37 at-bats.

When he was a young player working his way up through the minor leagues, the effervescent Sosa was regarded as a hitter with plenty of home run potential. But no one would have been brash enough to predict the kind of slugger the Chicago Cubs right fielder would become in the late 1990s.

Sammy Sosa was the first to accomplish back-to-back 60 homer seasons.

Sosa had hit more than 30 home runs in four different seasons since his first full year with the Cubs in 1993. Before 1998, however, his high had been 40 in 1996.

Originally signed by the Texas Rangers in 1985, then traded to the Chicago White Sox in 1989 and to the Cubs in 1992, the compact 6-foot, 210-pound slugger was prone to strikeouts. He fanned more than 170 times each season between 1997 and 1999. But the Dominican Republic native had emerged as a feared power-hitter, and by 1998 was one of the premier long-distance clouters in the National League.

There was, of course, another premier home run hitter in the National League by the name of McGwire. He and Sosa would become inextricably linked in what were to be two of the greatest home run races between two players that ever took place. McGwire and Sosa were rivals on the field. But as they battled back and forth through two spectacular seasons, they also became friends, each applauding the other's efforts.

"We are friends," Sosa said, "but that doesn't mean he will give me anything too easy. I'm just very happy every time Mark hits a home run. It doesn't really matter who wins the home run title."

While the two hit home runs with dramatic frequency, a whole nation watched. First in 1998 and then again in 1999, fans—who since the ill-conceived strike of 1994 had been staying away in droves from the game—once again began crowding back into the ballparks.

With baseball back in the spotlight, Sosa did his best to give the fans their money's worth. Few players ever performed with as much exuberance as Sammy, and few ever demonstrated such joy at hitting a home run. "The name of the game is home run," said Sosa, the National League's Most Valuable Player in 1998. "The people come to the park to see us hit them."

After the torrid race in 1998, Sosa and McGwire both started slowly in 1999. By early May, Sosa had hit just four home runs. But eventually he picked up the pace, and by the All-Star break in mid-July he had connected for 32 homers.

By September, Sosa had not only moved into the home run lead, but he had also reached 300 career homers while joining Hack Wilson as the only Cubs players to drive in 100 runs in five consecutive seasons. "I go out there every day and try to do the best I can," Sosa said. "If I hit a home run, I hit a home run."

Sosa, who had hit his 60th homer in 1998 on September 12 off Velerio De Los Santos of the Milwaukee Brewers in a 15–12 Cubs win, slumped in mid-September. After hitting home run number 59 on September 9, he went seven games without a four-bagger.

But the disease that occasionally afflicts every hitter was finally cured when Sammy faced the Brewers on a warm September afternoon at Wrigley Field. The Cubs were buried deep behind Milwaukee in the National League's Central Division cellar. But 39,304, including Sosa's wife, mother, and son, who was celebrating his second birthday, came out to watch anyway. They were there mainly to see Sosa.

With the Brewers leading 3–1 in the sixth inning, Sammy turned on a 2–2 pitch by Bere and drilled it over the center field wall for his 60th homer of the season. It was the fifth time he had homered off Milwaukee pitching in 1999, and the 17th time he had raked the Brewers for a four-bagger in two years.

After crossing the plate, Sosa pointed to the sky, then jogged to the dugout where he was warmly embraced by Cubs teammates. Moments later, he came back out of the dugout and, as fans cheered wildly, blew one of his trademark kisses to the crowd.

"I just wanted to get it done. I was getting a bit anxious at the plate," Sosa said later. "Everybody was waiting for this moment. They were all cheering for me. My emotions were getting pretty high.

"Nobody was thinking about another 60–home run season back in April. But now that it's happened, I'm real happy to have been able to come back and do it.. This is sort of unbelievable."

Cubs outfielders Henry Rodriguez and Roosevelt Brown remained in the dugout as Chicago players trotted onto the field to start the seventh inning, letting Sosa run out alone to the thundering cheers of the crowd. Sammy tipped his cap and waved toward the bleachers.

Sosa batted four more times in the game, getting a seventh-inning walk, a ninth-inning single, grounding out in the 11th, and fouling out in the 13th. His Cubs finally lost in the 14th inning as the Brewers scored three runs to win.

But history had been made. Sosa had done something twice that Babe Ruth, that Roger Maris, and that to that point Mark McGwire had only done once. McGwire, who stood four homers behind Sosa at the time, would, of course, soon reach 60 himself for the second straight year.

"Babe was the greatest player ever to play the game," Sosa told reporters. "For me, a guy from the Dominican Republic to be mentioned with him, it's a great feeling.

"I enjoyed this one more than last year," he added. "Of all the players who have played this game, for me to be the first one [to hit 60 home runs twice], makes me proud of myself."

The effort by Sosa, who earlier in the season had gone eight games without a home run, was not lost on others. "He's one of the game's real treasures," said Milwaukee manager Jim Lefebvre, a former Cubs skipper. "He did something nobody had ever done. Nobody worked harder than Sammy to do that."

Chicago batting coach and Hall of Famer Billy Williams was equally effusive. "It's tough enough to hit a baseball, but when you can hit 60 home runs two years in a row, that's just amazing," he said. "It's a great feat."

Sosa added home run number 61 the very next day when he smashed a two-run shot in the first inning off the Brewers' Hideo Nomo. The blow bounced into a car windshield beyond the left-field wall of Wrigley Field.

Sammy hit two more homers as the season came to a close, including a a sizzling line drive to deep left-center field against the Philadelphia Phillies' Anthony Shumaker at Veterans Stadium. Sosa seemed barely out of the batter's box when the ball left the park.

The final home run for Sosa came on the last day of the season in St. Louis. It gave him a final total of 63. But by that time, a hot streak by McGwire had vaulted the Cardinals slugger into the lead. McGwire finished the season with 65 homers to win the crown for the second year in a row.

"I'm happy," Sosa said. "I'm happy to share the home run race with Mark. I finished second, and I'm still happy."

Sosa finished the 20th century with 128 home runs in the final two years. Only McGwire hit more homers in two seasons. Although he kept coming out second best to McGwire in their torrid two-season battle, Sosa made at least one major mark on the record book. Sixty home runs two years in a row was a feat that Sammy was the first big league hitter ever to achieve.

Milwaukee	AB	R	H	RBI	Chicago	AB	R	H	RBI
Grissom, cf	7	1	1	0	Brown, cf	5	1	2	0
Loretta, 1b	5	0	1	0	Heredia, p	0	0	0	0
Cirillo, 3b	6	0	0	0	Ayala, p	0	0	0	0
Burnitz, rf	6	1	1	2	Alexander, ph	1	0	0	0
Belliard, 2b	6	1	1	1	Aguilera, p	0	0	0	0
Ochoa, lf	4	2	1	0	Liniak, 2b	1	0	0	0
Valentin, ss	5	2	1	0	Meyers, 2b	2	0	1	0
Cancel, c	3	0	1	2	Morandini, ph, 2b	3	0	0	0
Jenkins, ph	1	0	0	0	Grace, 1b	5	2	1	0
Wickman, p	0	0	0	0	Sosa, rf	6	1	2	1
Weathers, p	0	0	0	0	Rodriguez, lf	6	0	1	0
Mouton, ph	1	0	0	0	Sanders, p	0	0	0	0
Peterson, p	1	0	0	0	Andrews, 3b	5	0	1	2
Bere, p	2	0	1	0	Guthrie, p	0	0	0	0
Plunk, p	0	0	0	0	Porter, lf	1	0	0	0
Barker, ph	1	0	0	0	Nieves, ss	4	0	1	0
Roque, p	0	0	0	0	Hill, ph	0	0	0	0
Ramirez, p	0	0	0	0	Blauser, ss	2	0	0	0
M. Myers, p	0	0	0	0	Molina, c	2	0	0	0
Coppinger, p	0	0	0	0	Johnson, ph, cf	1	0	0	1
Greene, c	0	0	0	0	Bowie, p	2	0	1	0
Banks, ph, c	3	0	1	2	Gaetti, ph	1	0	0	0
					R. Myers, p	0	0	0	0
					Reed, ph, c	3	0	0	0
Totals	51	7	9	7		50	4	10	4

Milwaukee	1	0	0	2	0	0	0	0	1	0	0	0	0	3	**7**
Chicago	1	0	0	0	0	1	1	0	1	0	0	0	0	0	**4**

Milwaukee	IP	H	R	ER	BB	SO
Bere	5⅔	5	2	2	4	5
Plunk	⅓	0	0	0	0	0
Roque	⅔	0	1	1	1	1
Ramirez	0*	0	0	0	1	0
M. Myers	0†	0	0	0	1	0
Coppinger	1⅓	2	0	0	1	0
Wickman	1	1	1	1	3	2
Weathers	2	1	0	0	0	0
Peterson (W)	3	1	0	0	2	2

Chicago	IP	H	R	ER	BB	SO
Bowie	6	5	3	3	2	5
R. Myers	2	0	0	0	0	0
Heredia	0‡	1	1	1	0	4
Ayala	2	0	0	0	1	4
Guthrie (L)	2⅓	1	1	1	0	2
Sanders	⅔	2	2	2	1	1

*Pitched to one batter in seventh
†Pitched to one batter in seventh
‡Pitched to one batter in ninth

E–Cancel, Nieves. DP–Milwaukee 2. LOB–Milwaukee 6, Chicago 17. 2B–Grissom, Ochoa, Cancel, Nieves. 3B–Banks. HR–Belliard, Burnitz, Sosa. SB–Ochoa. WP–Bowie, Ayala. T–4:44. A-39,304.

Top 10 Homers in the All-Star Game

There is something terribly contradictory about an All-Star Game home run. On the one hand, coming as it does in what is actually just an exhibition game, it is essentially meaningless except in the context of the moment. On the other hand, as a feat that occurs in one of baseball's most celebrated events, it is magnified and glorified and afforded a special place in the galaxy of memorable home runs.

Because they did not occur during or have any bearing on regular or post-season play, we have chosen not to include All-Star Game home runs among the main group of baseball's most memorable home runs. They are cited instead in this special chapter.

That decision should not be construed, however, as an attempt to denigrate the significance of All-Star Game homers. Quite to the contrary, with the spotlight shining brightly, as it always does, on baseball's midsummer classic, there have been a number of home runs hit in that game that have been particularly noteworthy. Some stand out more than others. Some have carved a special place in baseball history. Here are the top 10:

Babe Ruth—July 6, 1933—Comiskey Park

It was the first All-Star Game, and it was an instant success. John McGraw was called out of retirement to manage against Connie Mack. Eleven future Hall of Famers were in the starting lineups. A crowd of 47,595 jammed every corner of Chicago's Comiskey Park. What could be more appropriate than Babe Ruth hitting the first home run? Baseball's most feared hitter wasted little time earning that distinction as he drilled a two-run homer in his second at-bat of the game. Coming in the third inning off Wild Bill Hallahan, the blow gave the American League the winning margin in a 4–2 victory. The 38-year-old New York Yankees star also made a sparkling catch in right field and added a single in his four trips to the plate in what turned out to be his next-to-last All-Star Game.

Ted Williams—July 8, 1941—Briggs Stadium

To date, no All-Star Game had gone down to the final inning to reach a conclusion. That changed at Detroit's Briggs Stadium when Ted Williams socked a two-out, three-run homer in the bottom of the ninth to give the American League a stunning 7–5 win. Arky Vaughan's two home runs in the seventh and eighth innings had given the National League a 5–3 lead entering the last inning. In the bottom of the ninth, with Claude Passeau on the mound for the Nationals, one-out singles by Ken Keltner and Joe Gordon and a walk to Cecil Travis loaded the bases before one run scored on Joe DiMaggio's force-out. Down to their last out and trailing, 5–4, the American League won as Williams drilled a Passeau fastball against the façade atop the right-field stands for what has stood as one of the most dramatic homers in All-Star Game history.

Ted Williams—July 9, 1946—Fenway Park

Travel restrictions imposed by World War II had forced cancellation of the 1945 All-Star Game. The National League may have wished the same had happened in 1946. In the most lopsided game up to that time, Ted Williams put on one of the most glittering performances in All-Star history, going 4-for-4 with two singles, two home runs, a walk, and five RBI to spark the American League to a 12–0 victory at Boston's Fenway Park. Williams hit a solo homer in the fourth inning. But the big blow for the Boston Red Sox slugger came in the eighth. Rip Sewell was the opposing pitcher. Few outside of the National League had ever seen his tantalizing and highly unusual blooper pitch. He tried one on Williams. Ted stepped forward—some said he moved in front of the batter's box—and laced the blooper into the right field bullpen for a three-run homer. It was the first four-bagger ever hit off Sewell's blooper

Red Schoendienst—July 11, 1950—Comiskey Park

No All-Star Game had ever gone extra innings before. And the National League had not won a game since 1944. But in one of the most event-filled All-Star Games ever played, Red Schoendienst's 14th-inning home run made the Nationals 4–3 winners at Comiskey Park. It was the Nationals' first win as a visiting team. During the game, Ted Williams broke an elbow crashing into the wall to make a catch in left field, Robin Roberts made his first of five All-Star starts over the next six years, and Larry Jansen pitched five brilliant innings of relief for the National League. The Nationals trailed 3–2 entering the ninth inning. Ralph Kiner sent the game into overtime with a clutch home run. Then, after four scoreless innings, the St. Louis Cardinals' Schoendienst, in his first at-bat of the game, walloped the first pitch from Ted Gray over the wall to send his team home with a stunning victory.

Stan Musial—July 12, 1955—County Stadium

After losing 12 of the first 17 All-Star Games, the National League had taken the upper hand. By 1955, they were in the midst of winning six of seven games. Thanks to the St. Louis Cardinals' Stan Musial, the surge was preserved at County Stadium in Milwaukee with another extra-inning home run. The clout came in the bottom of the 12th inning and climaxed a valiant comeback by the National League. The American League had built a 5–0 lead with the help of Mickey Mantle's 430-foot homer that sparked a four-run first inning off Robin Roberts. But the Nationals came back with five runs against Whitey Ford in the seventh and eighth innings. The score stayed knotted until the 12th when Musial, leading off the inning, slammed Frank Sullivan's first pitch for a game-winning homer

Stan Musial won the 1955 All-Star Game with a 12th-inning home run.

and a 6–5 National League win. Musial's clout was his fourth in what would become a record six All-Star Game home runs

Johnny Callison—July 7, 1964—Shea Stadium

It was another spectacular late-inning comeback. And another dramatic home run in the last inning. It happened at Shea Stadium in New York when Johnny Callison of the Philadelphia Phillies slammed a two-out, three-run homer in the bottom of the ninth inning to vault the National League to a stirring 7–4 decision. The win was the sixth in the last seven games for the Nationals, and finally pulled them even with the American League in the series with 17 victories apiece. Home runs by Billy Williams and Ken Boyer had given the NL a 2–1 lead in the fourth, but the AL had chipped away to go ahead, 4–3, in the seventh. That was still the score in

Johnny Callision got a boisterous welcome after hitting a game-winning home run in the 1964 All-Star Game.

the bottom of the ninth when Willie Mays singled, stole second, and scored on Orlando Cepeda's single. Then after a walk and two outs, Callison, a late-inning substitute, rocketed a Dick Radatz first-pitch fastball into the right-field seats to end the game.

Tony Perez—July 11, 1967—Anaheim Stadium

It was starting to seem like the National League had a monopoly on extra-inning home runs. Once again, the senior circuit won in dramatic fashion as the Cincinnati Reds' Tony Perez blasted a 15th-inning home run that delivered a 2–1 victory to the Nationals at California's one-year-old Anaheim Stadium. Twelve pitchers registered 30 strikeouts in the game. All the runs came on solo homers, with Dick Allen putting the NL on top in the second and Brooks Robinson tying the count in the sixth. There was no scoring again until the top of the 15th when Perez stepped to the plate facing Jim (Catfish) Hunter, hurling in his fifth inning of relief. With darkness closing in, Perez laced a one-strike pitch out of the park to put a decisive end to the longest All-Star Game ever played.

Reggie Jackson—July 13, 1971—Tiger Stadium

There have been other pinch-hit home runs in the rich history of the All-Star Game, but none quite rivaled the mammoth blast struck by Reggie Jackson of the Oakland Athletics in 1971. It didn't win a game. And it didn't earn special marks for its late-inning drama. All it did was travel some 520 feet and crash into a light tower high above Tiger Stadium's right-center-field roof. It was the longest All-Star Game homer ever hit. Jackson's gargantuan poke came off Dock Ellis with one man aboard in the third inning. Frank Robinson had already smacked a two-run homer in the same inning, thereby becoming the first player to hit All-Star homers for each league. Jackson, batting for Vida Blue, gave the American League a 4–3 lead with his blast, and helped to set up a 6–4 AL victory. The game featured six home runs and snapped an eight-game National League winning streak.

Mike Schmidt—August 19, 1981—Municipal Stadium

A players' strike had shut down baseball and forced cancellation of not only 50 days of the season but the All-Star Game as well. What better way to celebrate baseball's return than with an All-Star Game one day before the regular season resumed? The Philadelphia Phillies' Mike Schmidt provided the heroics. With a record crowd of 72,086 in attendance at Cleveland's Municipal Stadium and a record 56 players seeing action, the National League won its 10th straight midsummer classic on Schmidt's two-run homer in the eighth inning. The blow, coming off Rollie Fingers, overcame a 4–3 American League lead and carried the Nationals to a 5–4 verdict. Earlier, Gary Carter had belted a pair of solo homers and Dave Parker had jacked one out for the NL. But the National League still trailed in the game until Schmidt wiped out the deficit with a smash into the left-field stands.

Fred Lynn—July 6, 1983—Comiskey Park

Hard as it is to believe, it took 50 years for the All-Star Game to get its first grand-slam homer. Over that period, 53 games were played (two games were played each season from 1959 to 1962). The drought was finally broken when Fred Lynn of the California Angels socked a grand slam in the third inning of a 13–3 American League win at Comiskey Park. The homer, served up by Atlee Hammaker, capped a record seven-run inning in which the Americans also set a record with six hits, including a home run by Jim Rice. The win enabled the AL to gain its first victory after a record 11 straight All-Star Game losses. The National League had also won 19 of the previous 20 games. It was the largest margin of victory for a winning team since 1946. Lynn's blast was his fourth home run in All-Star Game competition.

Other Noteworthy Home Runs

When it comes to selecting baseball's most memorable home runs, the choices to some extent lie in the eye of the beholder. What is memorable to one person may not necessarily be as memorable to another.

In the preceding chapters, an attempt has been made to chronicle the 30 greatest home runs in baseball history. Those particular 30 are, of course, arbitrary choices. Some may be subject to debate.

That's because there have been numerous other noteworthy home runs. A good case could be made for the inclusion of some of them among the top 30. In the interest of paying at least some homage to those homers, too, here are what could be considered baseball's other memorable home runs (in feats performed more than once, only the first ones accomplished are included):

Ross Barnes of the Chicago White Stockings becomes the first National League player to hit a home run when he slugs an inside-the-park homer off Bill (Cherokee) Fisher of the Cincinnati Red Stockings at Cincinnati. The ball flew over the left fielder's head and into a row of horse-drawn carriages—May 2,1876.

Bobby Lowe of the Boston Beaneaters becomes the first major league player to hit four home runs in one game when he performs the feat in a 20–11 victory over Cincinnati at Boston. Two of Lowe's homers came in the third inning—May 30, 1894.

Ty Cobb of the Detroit Tigers clinches the American League home run title with an inside-the-park homer for his ninth four-bagger of the season. All nine of Cobb's homers were inside-the-parkers, making him the only player in the 20th century to win a home run crown without hitting a ball out of the park—September 13, 1909.

Ty Cobb won the 1909 home run crown without hitting a ball out of the park.

Harry Hooper homers in the top of the ninth inning of the fifth game to win the World Series for the Boston Red Sox. The blast produced a 5–4 victory over the Phillies at Philadelphia. It was Hooper's second homer of the game in a Series in which all but one of the five games were decided by one run—October 13, 1915.

Babe Ruth astounds baseball followers when he hits his 54th home run of the season off Dave Keefe of the Philadelphia Athletics on the final day of the campaign. In his first season with the New York Yankees, Ruth exceeds his previous record high set a year earlier by a whopping 25 homers. Coming at the beginning of the lively ball era, Ruth's 54 total was higher than the totals of all other American League teams—September 29, 1920.

Elmer Smith blasts the first grand-slam home run in World Series history in the first inning of a remarkable Game 5 at Cleveland. Hit off Burleigh Grimes, the homer leads the way to an 8–1 victory for the Cleveland Indians over the Brooklyn Dodgers. In the same game, the Indians' Jim Bagby became the first pitcher to hit a World Series home run and second baseman Bill Wambsganss pulled off the only unassisted triple play in Series history. Cleveland went on to win the Series, five games to two—October 10, 1920.

Casey Stengel of the New York Giants lumbers around the bases in the top of the ninth inning with the first inside-the-park home run in World Series history. It came in the first Series game ever played at Yankee Stadium, and it gave the Giants a 5–4 win over the New York Yankees. Two days after his two-out homer off Joe Bush, Stengel's solo homer gave the Giants a 1–0 triumph in Game 3. The Giants, however, lost the Series in six games—October 10, 1923.

Jim Bottomley slams a fourth-inning grand slam and a sixth-inning two-run homer while collecting six hits and driving in a major league record 12 runs to lead the St. Louis Cardinals to a 17–3 rout of the Brooklyn Robins at Ebbets Field. Bottomley also lashed two two-run singles and a run-scoring single and double—September 16, 1924.

Mule Haas of the Philadelphia Athletics hits a fly ball to center field that is lost in the sun by the Chicago Cubs' Hack Wilson and goes for a

Hack Wilson held the National League home run record for 68 years.

three-run, inside-the-park home run. The blow comes during the greatest one-inning explosion in World Series history and helps the A's overcome an 8–0 deficit with a 10-run seventh inning in Game 4 at Philadelphia. The A's go on to win,10–8, then clinch the Series in Game 5, 3–2, after Haas's two-run homer ties the score in the ninth—October 12, 1929.

Jack Quinn, who pitched in the majors from 1909 to 1933, becomes the oldest player ever to hit a big league home run when he drills a pitch by the St. Louis Browns' Chad Kimsey over the fence in the sixth inning of an 8–3 Philadelphia Athletics victory in the second game of a doubleheader at Shibe Park. Quinn, who got the win in relief, was just eight days shy of his 47th birthday. He hit eight homers during a 23-year big league career—June 27, 1930.

Hack Wilson of the Chicago Cubs slugs two home runs in the final game of the season to finish the year with a National League record 56 homers. The record stands for 68 years. Wilson's clouts led the Cubs to a 13–8 win over the Cincinnati Reds at Wrigley Field. In the game, Wilson also added to his RBI total, finishing with 190 for the season, a major league record that still stands—September 27, 1930.

Jimmie Foxx breaks a scoreless tie in the top of the ninth inning of the fifth game of the World Series with a two-run homer off Burleigh Grimes. The clout gives the Philadelphia Athletics a 2–0 victory over the St. Louis Cardinals at St. Louis and sets the stage for the A's second straight Series victory two days later in the sixth game—October 6, 1930.

Lou Gehrig makes baseball history by slugging his third grand-slam home run in four days. The record-setting belt led the New York Yankees to an 11–3 win over the Boston Red Sox in the first game of a doubleheader at Yankee Stadium. In the nightcap, Gehrig, en route to an American League–record 184 RBI, laced his sixth home run in six consecutive games in a 5–1 Yankee win—September 1, 1931.

Babe Ruth, playing with the Boston Braves, slams a 600-foot drive for the 714th and final home run of his storied career. The homer, Ruth's third of the day, is the first ever to clear the right-field roof at Pittsburgh's Forbes Field. Eight days later, the 40-year-old slugger retires as a player—May 25, 1935.

Tony Lazzeri becomes the first major leaguer to hit two grand slams in one game while leading the New York Yankees to a 25–2 bashing of the Philadelphia Athletics. Lazzeri also slugged a solo homer and a two-run triple to end the day at Shibe Park with an American League record 11 RBI. Lazzeri's home run outburst gave him a record seven home runs in four consecutive games—May 25, 1936.

Hank Greenberg socks two home runs at Briggs Stadium to lead the Detroit Tigers to a 7–4 victory over the New York Yankees in his final game before being inducted into the army. Greenberg, the first position player drafted for military duty in World War II, would spend more than four years in the service—May 6, 1941.

Jim Tobin becomes the only pitcher in baseball history to hit three home runs in one game when he bats and pitches the Boston Braves to a 6–5 win over the Chicago Cubs at Boston. One day earlier Tobin had hit a pinch-hit homer, giving him four round-trippers in five at-bats—May 13, 1942.

George McQuinn slugs a two-run, fourth-inning home run to give the St. Louis Browns a 2–1 victory over the St. Louis Cardinals in Game 1 of their first World Series appearance. The blow, coming off Mort Cooper at Sportsman's Park, was the only homer ever hit by a Browns player in the World Series—October 4, 1944.

Tommy Brown of the Brooklyn Dodgers homers off the Pittsburgh Pirates' Preacher Roe to become the youngest player ever to hit one out of the park in the big leagues. Brown, a wartime necessity who spent nine seasons in the majors, was just 17 years old—August 20, 1945.

Frankie Hayes, the Cleveland Indians catcher, clubs a ninth-inning home run as Bob Feller hurls a no-hitter to beat the New York Yankees, 1–0, at Yankee Stadium. Feller had just returned from nearly four years of military service. It was his second of three no-hitters. Three months later, having been sold to the Chicago White Sox, Hayes broke up another no-hit bid by Feller with a seventh-inning single—April 30, 1946.

Ted Williams foils the Boudreau Shift with an opposite-field, inside-the-park home run to left. The drive gives the Boston Red Sox a 1–0 victory over the Cleveland Indians and clinches the American League pennant for the Bosox. Cleveland manager Lou Boudreau, frustrated by the way Williams manhandled his pitchers, initiated the shift in an attempt to stop the Boston slugger. Still, Williams hit .400 against the shift that year, and his homer over left fielder Pat Seerey's head was the only inside-the-parker he ever hit—September 13, 1946.

Ralph Kiner drills two home runs to run his total to a major league record eight homers in four consecutive games in a Pittsburgh Pirates 4–3 win over the Boston Braves. Kiner, en route to winning or tying for seven straight National League home run titles, had hit three four-baggers the previous day—September 12, 1947.

Lou Boudreau sets a shining example as he laces two home runs to lead the Cleveland Indians to an 8–3 victory over the Boston Red Sox in a spe-

Ralph Kiner smacked eight homers in four games in 1947.

cial one-game playoff. The teams had ended the regular season in a tie for first place. Boudreau, the Cleveland manager, hit solo homers in the first off Denny Galehouse and in the fifth off Ellis Kinder while adding two singles. Kenny Keltner also hit a key homer for the Indians—October 4, 1948.

Tommy Henrich breaks up one of the finest pitching duels in World Series history with a home run in the bottom of the ninth inning to give the New York Yankees a 1–0 victory over the Brooklyn Dodgers in the opening game at Yankee Stadium. The blow, leading off the ninth, broke up a masterful battle between the Dodgers' Don Newcombe and the Yanks' Allie Reynolds, who pitched a two-hitter. It was only the fifth hit off Newcombe—October 5, 1949.

Bob Nieman of the St. Louis Browns makes an unprecedented major league debut by drilling home runs in his first two trips to the plate. Nieman, who had just been brought up from the Texas League, slammed a two-run homer in the second and another two-run blast in the third. Both were hit off Mickey McDermott, came on the first pitch, and flew over the

Jackie Robinson homered to send the 1951 Dodgers into a special playoff.

Green Monster at Boston's Fenway Park. Despite Nieman's lusty hitting, the Browns lost to the Boston Red Sox, 9–6—September 14, 1951.

Jackie Robinson comes back from being knocked out to homer in the 14th inning of the last game of the season to give the Brooklyn Dodgers a 9–8 victory over the Philadelphia Phillies and a tie for first place in the National League. In the ninth inning, Robinson had saved the game for the Dodgers with a sensational diving catch of Eddie Waitkus's two-out, bases-loaded line drive. Robinson was knocked out on the play as he fell heavily to the Shibe Park turf. Dodgers euphoria was short-lived as they lost to the New York Giants in a three-game playoff—September 30, 1951.

Stan Musial smashes a record five home runs in a doubleheader at St. Louis. The Cardinals slugger swatted three homers in a 10–6 win over the New York Giants in the opener, with his three-run dinger in the eighth snapping a 6–6 tie. He added two more round-trippers in a 9–7 loss in the nightcap, ending the day with six hits and nine RBI—May 2, 1954.

Joe Adcock of the Milwaukee Braves has the biggest offensive outburst in big league history as he sets a major league record with 18 total bases in one game. He did it with four home runs and a double while leading his team to a 15–7 triumph over the Brooklyn Dodgers at Ebbets Field—July 31, 1954.

Dale Long, a journeyman first baseman with the Pittsburgh Pirates, makes baseball history with his eighth home run in eight straight games. The homer is hit off Carl Erskine in the fourth inning of a game at Pittsburgh, and gives the Pirates the margin of victory in a 3–2 win over the Brooklyn Dodgers—May 28, 1956.

Mickey Mantle concludes a banner season with a solo homer in the 10th inning to give the New York Yankees a 3–2 win over the Chicago White Sox and the American League pennant. The blow, coming against Billy Pierce, was Mantle's 50th homer of the season. Mantle would go on to win the Triple Crown (.353–52–130)—September 18, 1956.

Hank Aaron snaps a 2–2 tie with a two-run homer in the bottom of the 11th inning off Billy Muffett of the St. Louis Cardinals. The blow gives the Milwaukee Braves a 4–2 victory at County Stadium and clinches the club's first pennant since it left Boston—September 23, 1957.

Jim Gentile of the Baltimore Orioles becomes the first batter to hit grand-slam homers in consecutive at-bats when he pounds four-baggers in the first and second innings against the Minnesota Twins. The first homer came against Pedro Ramos, the second off Paul Giel in a 13–5 Orioles victory. Gentile drove in a club-record nine runs in the game at Metropolitan Stadium—May 9, 1961.

Willie Mays, who had hit his first home run off Warren Spahn in 1951, smacks a dramatic solo shot in the bottom of the 16th inning to break up a scoreless duel between the San Francisco Giants' Juan Marichal and Spahn of the Milwaukee Braves. Both pitchers worked all 16 innings of the 1–0 classic at San Francisco—July 2, 1963.

Johnny Lewis spoils a magnificent no-hit bid by the Cincinnati Reds' Jim Maloney with an 11th-inning home run that gives the last-place New

Willie Mays hit a game-winning homer in his first game with the Mets.

York Mets a stunning 1–0 victory. Lewis, who had struck out three times in the game, led off the 11th by hitting a pitch over the center field wall at Crosley Field. Maloney struck out 18 batters in the game—June 14, 1965.

Leo Cardenas reverses Jim Maloney's no-hit heartbreak with a 10th-inning home run off the foul pole at Wrigley Field to give the Cincinnati Reds a 1–0 victory over the Chicago Cubs. Maloney goes all 10 innings without giving up a hit while striking out 12 and walking a no-hit record 10—August 19, 1965.

Tony Cloninger becomes the first National League player and the only pitcher to hit two grand-slam homers in one game as his two blasts lead the Milwaukee Braves to a 17–3 win over the San Francisco Giants at Candlestick Park. Cloninger ended the game with a record for pitchers of nine RBI—July 3, 1966.

Rick Wise of the Philadelphia Phillies hits two home runs and pitches a no-hitter in a 4–0 victory over the Cincinnati Reds at Crosley Field. No pitcher in history had ever hit two homers while hurling a no-hitter. Wise drove in three runs with his fifth- and eighth-inning blasts. It was the second time that season that Wise homered twice in one game—June 23, 1971.

Cesar Cedeno of the Houston Astros hits what is considered the shortest grand slam in major league history when his 200-foot fly ball falls safely as Los Angeles Dodgers second baseman Jim Lefebvre and right fielder Bill Buckner collide while trying to make the catch. As the two Dodgers lie on the ground, Cedeno circles the bases with an inside-the-park grand slam, helping the Astros to a 9–3 victory—September 2, 1971.

Willie Mays makes a triumphant return to New York when he hits a game-winning home run in his first game with the New York Mets. The fifth-inning clout off Don Carrithers gives the Mets the winning margin in a 5–4 victory over Mays' old team, the San Francisco Giants. The 41-year-old slugger had been a legend in New York before his Giants left in 1958—May 14, 1972.

Nate Colbert of the San Diego Padres ties a major league record with five home runs in a doubleheader. In the process, he sets a National League mark with 13 RBI in two games as the Padres sweep the Atlanta Braves, 9–0 and 11–7. Included in the barrage were a three-run homer and a solo shot in the first game, and a grand slam and two two-run homers in the nightcap—August 1, 1972.

Gene Tenace, a utility man who hit just five home runs all season, slams homers off Gary Nolan in his first two World Series at-bats, driving in all the runs as the Oakland Athletics defeat the Cincinnati Reds, 3–2, in the first game. Tenace hit four homers in the Series and doubled home the winning run in the A's 3–2 clincher in Game 7—October 14, 1972.

Joe Rudi smashes a leadoff home run in the top of the seventh inning to give the Oakland A's a 3–2 victory over the Los Angeles Dodgers in the fifth and deciding game of the World Series. Rudi's game-winning belt was served up by Mike Marshall, who during the season had appeared in a record 106 games. It came as the A's won the final three games of the Series—October 17, 1974.

Hank Aaron, wearing the uniform of the Milwaukee Brewers, hits his 755th and final home run back in the town where he had started his career 22 years earlier. Baseball's all-time home run king connected off Dick Drago of the California Angels—July 20, 1976.

Bucky Dent, batting ninth in the lineup, slams a three-run, seventh-inning homer into the left-field screen at Fenway Park to fuel a four-run rally that helped the New York Yankees gain a 5–4 victory over the Boston Red Sox in a special one-game playoff. The two teams had ended the regular season tied for first place in the AL East. With Dent's homer off Mike Torrez, New York overcame a 2–0 deficit and gained a 3–2 lead. One more run in the seventh and one in the eighth offset two runs in the bottom of the eighth by the Red Sox, who had led in the race by four games in early September—October 2, 1978.

Mike Schmidt smashes a two-run homer in the 11th inning to give the Philadelphia Phillies a 6–4 victory over the Montreal Expos and the National League East Division championship. The swat off Stan Bahnsen ended a nearly four-hour marathon that had begun after a three-hour rain delay on the next-to-last day of the season, and it propelled the Phillies on the way to their only World Series victory—October 4, 1980.

Rick Monday crushes the hopes of the Montreal Expos when he pokes a two-out, ninth-inning home run in the fifth game of the National League LCS to give the Los Angeles Dodgers a 2–1 win and the pennant. The Dodgers were down two games to one before winning the last two games of the playoff. Monday's homer off Steve Rogers came in 40-degree temperatures at Montreal—October 19,1981.

George Brett of the Kansas City Royals hits a two-out, two-run homer in the top of the ninth inning off Goose Gossage to give his team an apparent 5–4 lead over the New York Yankees at Yankee Stadium. Upon examining Brett's bat, however, umpire Tim McClelland nullified the home run and called Brett out, ruling the bat was illegal because pine tar extended too far up its handle. While Brett flew into a rage, the Yankees were awarded a 4–3 win. Four days later, the ruling was reversed by American League president Lee McPhail. The game was resumed later with the Royals tallying a 5–4 win—July 24, 1983.

Harold Baines drills a bases-empty home run to end a 25-inning, eight hour and six minute marathon in which the Chicago White Sox beat the Milwaukee Brewers, 7–6, at Comiskey Park. The game had been suspended after 17 innings the previous night because of an American League curfew with the teams tied at 3–3. When it was resumed before the regularly scheduled game the next night, each team scored three runs in the 21st inning before Baines lashed his game winner off Chuck Porter, ending the longest game in terms of time elapsed in major league history—May 5, 1984.

Kirk Gibson wallops two home runs into the upper deck at Tiger Stadium in Game 5 of the World Series to lead the Detroit Tigers to an 8–4 victory and their first championship since 1968. Facing the San Diego Padres, Gibson hit a two-run homer off Mark Thurmond in the first inning. Then he clinched the win and the Series for the Tigers with a three-run blast off Goose Gossage in the eighth—October 14, 1984.

Ozzie Smith, a switch-hitter more noted for his defense, hits his first left-handed home run in more than 3,000 at-bats to give the St. Louis Cardinals a 3–2 victory over the Los Angeles Dodgers in the fifth game of the National League playoffs. The blow, coming off Tom Niedenfuer in the bottom of the ninth inning, was only the 14th homer of Smith's major league career. It set the stage for a Cardinals pennant-clinching victory the next day—October 14, 1985.

Dave Henderson knocks a two-out, two-run homer in the bottom of the ninth of the fifth game to keep his Boston Red Sox alive in the American League playoffs. With a three-games-to-one lead, the California Angels needed just one out to go to the World Series. But the visiting Red Sox scored four times in the ninth inning with Henderson's homer off Donnie Moore giving them a 6–5 lead. The Angels tied the score in the bottom of the ninth, but Boston won in the 11th, 7–6, then triumphed in the next two games to complete one of the most dramatic comebacks in LCS history—October 12, 1986.

Don Mattingly of the New York Yankees homers over the left-center-field wall in the fourth inning to extend his streak to eight straight games with a home run. The spree tied a major league record. Mattingly hit 10 home runs during the eight games. His last one, coming off Jose Guzman, failed to prevent a 7–2 Yankees loss to the Texas Rangers at Arlington Field—July 18, 1987.

Mark McGwire sets a major league record for a rookie when he blasts his 39th home run of the season in the sixth inning off Don Sutton of the California Angels. The blow helps the visiting Oakland Athletics to a 7–6 victory and puts McGwire one ahead of former co–record holders Wally Berger of the Boston Braves (1930) and Frank Robinson of the Cincinnati Reds (1956). McGwire finished the season with a league-leading 49 homers—August 14, 1987.

Ken Griffey, Sr. and Jr., hit back-to-back homers against Kirk McCaskill in the first inning of the Seattle Mariners' 7–6 loss to the California Angeles. It was the only time in baseball history that father and son homered in the same major league game—September 14, 1990.

Kirby Puckett, with his team facing extinction, belts a home run leading off the bottom of the 11th inning to give the Minnesota Twins a 4–3 victory over the Atlanta Braves in the sixth game of the World Series. The blow, hit off Charlie Leibrandt, pulled the Twins even in the Series at three wins apiece. Earlier in the game, Puckett had climbed the wall in center to make a spectacular catch. Minnesota went on clinch the Series the following day with a 1–0 triumph—October 26, 1991.

Carlos Baerga of the Cleveland Indians becomes the first switch-hitter to homer from both sides of the plate in the same inning when he launches two bombs in the seventh inning of a 15–5 victory over the New York Yankees at Cleveland. Baerga hit a two-run homer from the right side of the plate off Steve Howe. Six runs later, he touched Steve Farr for a solo shot batting from the left side of the plate. It was the 92nd time a player had homered from both sides of the plate in the same game, but the first time it happened in the same inning—April 8, 1993.

Dave Justice, having been booed heavily after criticizing Atlanta fans, turns the crowd around with a sixth-inning solo homer that gives the Braves a 1–0 victory in Game 6 of the World Series. The homer off Jim Poole delivers the only championship to Atlanta in a hard-fought Series with the Cleveland Indians—October 28, 1995.

Mark McGwire breaks the all-time home run record with his 62nd round-tripper of the season as the St. Louis Cardinals beat the Chicago Cubs, 6–3, at Busch Stadium. The shot, served up by Steve Trachsel, snapped the 37-year-old record of 61 set in 1961 by Roger Maris, whose four children were in attendance. McGwire went on to finish the season with a remarkable 70 homers—September 8, 1998.

Sammy Sosa of the Chicago Cubs does something no other player has ever done before when he hits his 66th home run of the season. The blow off Jose Lima of the Houston Astros came in a 6–2 Cubs loss at the Astrodome. In becoming the first player ever to hit that many home runs, Sosa briefly took over the major league home run lead before Mark McGwire came back to catch him a few hours later—September 25, 1998.

Wade Boggs becomes the only player ever to homer on his 3,000th hit when he slugs a Chris Haney pitch over the right-field wall at Tropicana Field. The two-run homer came just 20 miles from where the Tampa Bay Devil Rays infielder grew up. Boggs is the 23rd player to reach 3,000 hits in a career. His sixth-inning homer, however, failed to avert a 15–10 Devil Rays loss to the Cleveland Indians – August 7, 1999.

All-Time Home Run Leaders

500 Or More Career Home Runs

		HR	Years Played
1.	Hank Aaron	755	23
2.	Babe Ruth	714	22
3.	Willie Mays	660	22
4.	Frank Robinson	586	21
5.	Harmon Killebrew	573	22
6.	Reggie Jackson	563	21
7.	Mike Schmidt	548	18
8.	Mickey Mantle	536	18
9.	Jimmie Foxx	534	20
10.	Mark McGwire	522	13
11.	Willie McCovey	521	22
	Ted Williams	521	19
13.	Ernie Banks	512	19
	Eddie Mathews	512	17
15.	Mel Ott	511	22
16.	Eddie Murray	504	21

50 or More Home Runs in One Season

	HR	Year
Mark McGwire, St. Louis Cardinals	70	1998
Sammy Sosa, Chicago Cubs	66	1998
Mark McGwire, St. Louis Cardinals	65	1999
Sammy Sosa, Chicago Cubs	63	1999
Roger Maris, New York Yankees	61	1961
Babe Ruth, New York Yankees	60	1927

50 or More Home Runs in One Season (continued)

	HR	Year
Babe Ruth, New York Yankees	59	1921
Jimmie Foxx, Philadelphia Athletics	58	1932
Hank Greenberg, Detroit Tigers	58	1938
Mark McGwire, Oakland Athletics, St. Louis Cardinals	58	1997
Hack Wilson, Chicago Cubs	56	1930
Ken Griffey, Jr., Seattle Mariners	56	1997
Ken Griffey, Jr., Seattle Mariners	56	1998
Babe Ruth, New York Yankees	54	1920
Babe Ruth, New York Yankees	54	1928
Ralph Kiner, Pittsburgh Pirates	54	1949
Mickey Mantle, New York Yankees	54	1961
Mark McGwire, Oakland Athletics	52	1996
Mickey Mantle, New York Yankees	52	1956
Willie Mays, San Francisco Giants	52	1965
George Foster, Cincinnati Reds	51	1977
Ralph Kiner, Pittsburgh Pirates	51	1947
Johnny Mize, New York Giants	51	1947
Jimmie Foxx, Boston Red Sox	50	1938
Albert Belle, Cleveland Indians	50	1995
Brady Anderson, Baltimore Orioles	50	1996
Greg Vaughn, San Diego Padres	50	1998

Four Home Runs in One Game

Bobby Lowe, Boston Beaneaters, May 30, 1894
Ed Delahanty, Philadelphia Phillies, July 13, 1896
Lou Gehrig, New York Yankees, June 3, 1932
Chuck Klein, Philadelphia Phillies, July 10, 1936 (10 Innings)
Pat Seerey, Chicago White Sox, July 18, 1948 (11 innings)
Gil Hodges, Brooklyn Dodgers, August 31, 1950
Joe Adcock, Milwaukee Braves, July 31, 1954
Rocky Colavito, Cleveland Indians, June 10, 1959
Willie Mays, San Francisco Giants, April 30, 1961

Mike Schmidt, Philadelphia Phillies, April 17, 1976 (10 innings)
Bob Horner, Atlanta Braves, July 6, 1986
Mark Whiten, Cleveland Indians, September 7, 1993

Two Grand Slams in One Game

Tony Lazzeri, New York Yankees, May 24, 1936
Jim Tabor, Boston Red Sox, July 4, 1939
Rudy York, Boston Red Sox, July 27, 1946
Jim Gentile, Baltimore Orioles, May 9, 1961
Tony Cloninger, Atlanta Braves, July 3, 1966
Jim Northrup, Detroit Tigers, June 24, 1968
Frank Robinson, Baltimore Orioles, June 26, 1970
Robin Ventura, Chicago White Sox, September 4, 1995
Chris Hoiles, Baltimore Orioles, August 14, 1998
Fernando Tatis, St. Louis Cardinals, April 23, 1999
Nomar Garciaparra, Boston Red Sox, May 10, 1999

Sources

Books

Aaron, Hank. *If I Had a Hammer.* HarperCollins: 1991.

The Baseball Encyclopedia, 8th ed. Macmillan: 1990.

Caruso, Gary. *The Braves Encyclopedia.* Temple University Press: 1995.

Creamer, Roger W. *Babe.* Penguin Books: 1983.

Eisenbath, Mike. *The Cardinals Encyclopedia.* Temple University Press: 1999.

Gallagher, Mark. *The Yankees Encyclopedia.* Leisure Press: 1982.

Greenberg, Hank, and Ira Berkow. *The Story of My Life.* Times Books: 1989.

Holtzman, Jerome, and George Vass. *The Chicago Cubs Encyclopedia.* Temple University Press: 1997.

Honig, Donald. *Power Hitters,* The Sporting News: 1989.

Lindberg, Richard C. *The White Sox Encyclopedia.* Temple University Press: 1997.

Reichler, Joseph. *Baseball's Great Moments.* The Sporting News: 1983.

Reidenbaugh, Lowell. *Baseball's Greatest Games.* The Sporting News: 1986.

Reidenbaugh, Lowell. *Baseball's 25 Greatest Pennant Races.* The Sporting News: 1986.

Romanowski, Jerome. *The Mackmen.* Author: 1979.

Salant, Nathan. *Superstars, Stars and Just Plain Heroes.* Stein and Day: 1982.

Schneider, Russ. *The Cleveland Indians Encyclopedia.* Temple University Press: 1996.

The Scrapbook History of Baseball. Bobbs-Merrill: 1975.

Smith, Ron. *Chronicle of Baseball.* The Sporting News: 1993.

Sullivan, George, and John Powers. *The Yankees: An Illustrated History.* Temple University Press: 1997.

Total Baseball, 6th ed. Total Sports: 1999.

Westcott, Rich. *Diamond Greats.* Meckler Books: 1988.

Westcott, Rich. *Mike Schmidt.* Chelsea House: 1995.

Westcott, Rich. *Phillies '93: An Incredible Season.* Temple University Press: 1994.

Westcott, Rich, and Frank Bilovsky. *The New Phillies Encyclopedia.* Temple University Press: 1993.

Williams, Ted. *My Turn at Bat.* Simon & Schuster: 1969.

Newspapers

Baltimore Sun

Chicago Tribune

New York Times

Philadelphia Inquirer

St. Louis Post-Dispatch

Photograph Credits

Pages 3, 8, 21, 27, 41, 55, 78, 84, 95, 118, 130, 146, 172: National Baseball Hall of Fame Library, Cooperstown, New York

Pages 14, 60, 64, 108, 134, 192, 193, 198, 200, 203, 204: From the collection of Rich Westcott

Page 33: Courtesy of Tony Zonca

Pages 49, 90: Urban Archives, Temple University, Philadelphia, Pennsylvania

Pages 72, 102: Courtesy of George Sullivan

Page 124: New York Yankees

Pages 140, 176: St. Louis Cardinals

Page 154: Los Angeles Dodgers

Page 159: Toronto Blue Jays

Page 165: Courtesy of Bob Brown

Page 182: Photo by Stephen J. Carrera

Page 206: Photo by Bob Bartosz